Key Stage 4 / GCSE

On Course

Maths
Intermediate and Higher Tiers
. . . .
Summary and Practice Book
WITH FULL ANSWERS

Stanley Thornes (Publishers) Ltd   **Paul Metcalf, Liz Hamilton and Anne Haworth**

Introduction

This book has been written by experienced examiners and is endorsed by AQA for the following syllabuses in GCSE Mathematics

- NEAB GCSE Mathematics Syllabus A (1131)
- NEAB GCSE Mathematics Syllabus B (1132)
- SEG GCSE Mathematics Syllabus 2510T
- SEG GCSE Mathematics Syllabus 2510X

How to use this book

This book has been written to help you prepare for the Intermediate/Higher tier of your GCSE examination in Mathematics.

The book is divided into 18 short clear topics that cover attainment targets Ma 2 to Ma 4. The topics are grouped into four sections headed Number, Algebra, Shape, space and measures and Handling data.

Each colour-coded topic contains material divided into:

- **Intermediate work** – work covering grades D/E that appears on the Intermediate tier only

- **Intermediate/Higher work** – work covering grades B/C that appears on the Intermediate and Higher tiers

- **Higher work** – work covering grades A*/A that appears on the Higher tier only

For each of these levels there is a **Summary** and a **Practice Exercise**.

1 The Summary page tells you all the important facts you need to know for the different tiers. The summary pages are colour coded according to tier.

2 The Summary page is divided into different headings, some of which are revisited later in the section.

3 Additional notes are given in the margin and you may wish to add your own notes if you feel they are important.

4 Important words and formulae are printed in **bold** type.

5 Worked examples are given under the heading 'Like this'.

6 The Practice Exercise is designed to test and develop your understanding of the work from the Summary page. Practice Exercises are also colour coded according to tier.

7 You should answer the questions in the shaded areas or else in the column at the right-hand side of the page.

8 Answers to the Practice Exercises are included at the back of the book.

Remember that if you are entered for the Intermediate Tier then you do not have to cover work from the Higher Tier Only section. Similarly, if you are entered for the Higher Tier then you do not have to cover work from the Intermediate Tier Only section, although this work may be useful background material for you

At the end of each topic there is a set of **Examination Questions** for you to work through.

9 The Examination Questions are divided into the same tiers as the Summaries and Practice Exercises. They are also colour-coded according to tier.

10 The questions are included to give you experience of answering the type of questions which will be on the SEG and NEAB examination papers.

11 Where you see the 'non-calculator' symbol then you must not use a calculator. You can use your calculator for all other questions, but it is a good idea to manage without it where possible.

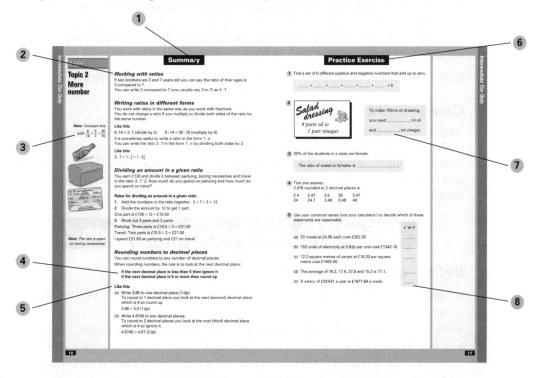

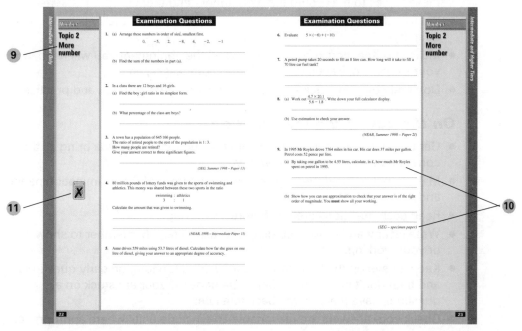

Assessment

The GCSE Mathematics syllabus is assessed at three overlapping tiers:

- Foundation tier – covering grades D, E, F and G
- Intermediate tier – covering grades B, C, D and E
- Higher tier – covering grades A*, A, B and C

Within each tier, the syllabus content is divided into four attainment targets with the following weightings:

- Ma 1   Using and applying mathematics   20%
- Ma 2   Number and algebra   40%
- Ma 3   Shape, space and measure   20%
- Ma 4   Handling data   20%

Written papers

For your GCSE examination you will be required to take two written papers covering attainment targets Ma 2 to Ma 4 (worth 80% of the overall mark). You will not be allowed to use a calculator on the first written paper, although you will be expected to have a calculator for the second paper.

Both papers may assess any topic in the subject content for the tier.

Coursework

All candidates are required to carry out investigations and practical tasks during KS4. The GCSE examination will test your ability to use and apply mathematics (MA 1) through coursework set and marked by the centre (SEG Syllabus 2510T and NEAB Syllabus A), or coursework set and marked by the board (SEG Syllabus 2510X) or a terminal examination (NEAB Syllabus B).

Preparing for the examination

Before the examination

- Get a copy of the syllabus document and identify the topics you need to work on.
- Read through the Summary pages of this book and make notes.
- Work through the Practice Exercises and Examination Questions and check your answers. Make a note of any mistakes you make and revisit these topics to make sure that you understand them.
- Put together a revision timetable and remember that quality is better than quantity!
- Make sure that you know how to use all the equipment you will need in your exam, e.g. calculator, protractor, compasses, etc.
- Don't rely on good luck – there is no substitute for revision and practice.

On the day of the examination

- Get to the examination in plenty of time and make sure you bring all the correct equipment you need with you.
- Make sure you read the instructions on the front of the examination paper and answer **all** the questions.
- Read each question carefully before answering.
- Write clearly and draw your diagrams accurately. Remember to show all of your working.
- Keep an eye on the time so you don't spend too long on early questions and then don't have time to finish the paper. If your are stuck on a question, leave it and come back to it later.
- Check your answers are reasonable and include units where appropriate.

Contents

Number

Algebra

Shape, Space and Measures

Handling Data

Topic 1

The rules of number

Note: Remember to cancel your fractions down where possible.

Changing fractions to decimals

To change fractions to decimals you divide the numerator by the denominator. Easy!

Like this

$\frac{3}{8} = 3 \div 8 = 0.375$

Changing decimals to fractions

All you have to remember is your decimal place values!

Like this

$0.2 = \frac{2}{10} = \frac{1}{5}$ and

$0.002 = \frac{2}{1000} = \frac{1}{500}$

Adding and subtracting fractions

To add or subtract fractions you first find a common denominator.

Like this

$1\frac{2}{5} + 2\frac{1}{4} = 1\frac{8}{20} + 2\frac{5}{20} = 3\frac{13}{20}$

As the common denominator of 5 and 4 is $5 \times 4 = 20$

Changing fractions or decimals into percentages

All you have to do is multiply the fraction or decimal by 100.

Like this

$\frac{5}{8} = \frac{5}{8} \times 100\% = 62.5\%$

$0.39 = 0.39 \times 100\% = 39\%$

Percentage changes

To find a percentage change you first have to find the actual increase/decrease or profit/loss.

Like this

(a) A washing machine is advertised at £450 plus VAT at $17\frac{1}{2}\%$. What is the cost of the washing machine?

VAT is $17\frac{1}{2}\%$ of £450 $= \dfrac{17.5}{100} \times £450 = £78.75$

Cost of washing machine $= £450 + £78.75 = £528.75$

(b) After one year a car which cost £15 596.00 is sold at a loss of 7%. What is the selling price?

Loss is 7% of £15 596.00 $= \dfrac{7}{100} \times £15\,596 = £1091.72$

Price of car after one year is £15 596.00 $-$ £1091.72 $=$ £14 504.28

Writing one quantity as a percentage of another

To find one quantity as a percentage of another you first have to find one quantity as a fraction of the other – then multiply the fraction by 100 to give a percentage.

Like this

I spend £104.50 on a new watch and then sell it for £90. What is my percentage loss?

Loss $=$ £104.50 $-$ £90 $=$ £14.50

Fraction is $\dfrac{£14.50}{£104.50}$

Percentage is $\dfrac{£14.50}{£104.50} \times 100\% = 13.9\%$ (approximately)

Note: Remember to put each quantity in the same units.

Practice Exercise

1 Find numbers for the blanks so that the lists are in order of size.

(a) 47, ..., ..., 48

(b) 2.3, ..., ..., 2.4

(c) 0.25, ..., ..., 0.267

(d) 0.037, ..., ..., 0.043

2 Match the numbers in Column 1 with those in Column 2.

Column 1	Column 2
0.3	$\frac{57}{100}$
$\frac{1}{4}$	$\frac{4}{5}$
57%	0.22
0.15	30%
0.8	0.25
22%	$\frac{3}{20}$

3 Choose an instruction from the list to put into each of the boxes a–c.

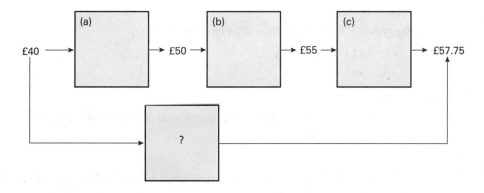

Instructions

increase by 20%

increase by 5%

increase by 10%

increase by 25%

Explain why the answer in the box marked '?' is not the same as the sum of boxes a, b and c.

Topic 1
The rules of number

Note: Convert back to mixed numbers when you have finished.

Multiplying fractions

To multiply two fractions you must remember to make them into improper fractions and cancel where possible.

Like this

(a) $\dfrac{4}{3} \times \dfrac{1}{11} = \dfrac{4 \times 1}{3 \times 11} = \dfrac{4}{33}$

(b) $1\dfrac{3}{5} \times 2\dfrac{1}{4} = \dfrac{\overset{2}{8}}{5} \times \dfrac{9}{\underset{1}{4}} = \dfrac{18}{5} = 3\dfrac{3}{5}$

Dividing fractions

Remember to turn the 'divide' fraction upside down and then multiply.

Like this

$1\dfrac{3}{5} \div 1\dfrac{1}{3} = \dfrac{8}{5} \div \dfrac{4}{3} = \dfrac{\overset{2}{8}}{5} \times \dfrac{3}{\underset{1}{4}} = \dfrac{6}{5} = 1\dfrac{1}{5}$

Finding a percentage change

An alternative method to find a percentage change uses a single multiplier.

Like this

(a) A washing machine is advertised at £450 plus VAT at $17\frac{1}{2}$%. What is the cost of the washing machine?

The new cost of the washing machine is

$117\frac{1}{2}$% (100% + $17\frac{1}{2}$%) of £450 $= \dfrac{117.5}{100} \times £450 = £528.75$

(b) After one year a car which cost £15 596.00 is sold at a loss of 7%. What is the selling price?

The selling price is 93% (100% − 7%) of £15 596.00

$= \dfrac{93}{100} \times £15\,596 = £14\,504.28$

Backwards percentages

In these questions you are given the actual increased or decreased quantity and have to find the **original** quantity.

Note: 100% is the original amount.

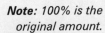

Like this

(a) In a box of chocolates 35% of the chocolates are soft centred. I ate all 21 soft centred-chocolates. How many chocolates were in the original selection?

35% of number of chocolates is 21

1% of number of chocolates is $\frac{21}{35}$ (dividing by 35 to find 1%)

100% of number of chocolates is $\frac{21}{35} \times 100$ (multiplying by 100 to find 100%)

Original number of chocolates is $\frac{21}{35} \times 100 = 60$

(b) In the sales all goods had a reduction of 25%. What was the original price of a mug whose sale price was 60p?

Reduction!   Sale price is 75% (100% − 25%)

So   75% of the price of a mug is 60p

     1% of the price of a mug is $\frac{60}{75}$p   (dividing by 75 to find 1%)

100% of the price of a mug is $\frac{60}{75} \times 100$ (multiplying by 100 to find 100%)

Original price is $\frac{60}{75} \times 100 = 80$p

Practice Exercise

1 Find a fraction whose value is between $\frac{2}{3}$ and $\frac{3}{4}$

2 Which of these are correct?
To increase an amount by 15% you multiply by:

(a) 0.15 (b) 1.15 (c) $\frac{100}{15}$ (d) $\frac{115}{100}$ (e) 1.5

3 The washing machine on the opposite page cost £528.75 including 17.5% VAT.

Show how to find the pre-VAT price of £450.

....

....

....

....

....

4 Which of these are correct?

450 g as a percentage of 2 kg is:

(a) $\frac{450}{200}\%$

(b) $\frac{450}{2000} \times 100\%$

(c) $\frac{450}{100} \times 2\%$

(d) $\frac{45\,000}{2000}\%$

(e) $22\frac{1}{2}\%$

(f) $\frac{450}{2} \times 100$

1 Answer ....

2 Answer ....

....

4 Answer ....

....

....

Number

Topic 1
The rules of number

Note: For a fraction with two recurring numbers you multiply by 100 (i.e. 10^2)

For a fraction with three recurring numbers you multiply by 1000 (i.e. 10^3)...

Note: An integer is a positive or negative counting number (a whole number).

Recurring decimals

Recurring decimals are rational numbers and can all be written as fractions.

Like this

Express $0.\dot{4}$ as a fraction
$$10 \times \text{fraction} = 4.444\,444\,444\ldots \qquad \text{(multiplying the fraction by 10)}$$
$$1 \times \text{fraction} = 0.444\,444\,444\,4$$

Subtracting these $\qquad 9 \times \text{fraction} = 4 \qquad (4.444\,444\,444 - 0.444\,444\,444\,4)$
$$\text{fraction} = \tfrac{4}{9} \qquad \text{(dividing both sides by 9)}$$
so $0.\dot{4} = \tfrac{4}{9}$

Working with irrational numbers

An irrational number is a number which cannot be written in the form $\dfrac{p}{q}$ where p and q are integers.

Other irrational numbers include π, $\sqrt{2}$, $\sqrt{3}$, $6^{1/2}$, $\sqrt[3]{4}$, $\sqrt[3]{7}$ and $12^{1/3}$ (the list includes all the square roots and cube roots which 'do not work out').

Multiplying and dividing roots

You can multiply and divide roots using the fact that $\sqrt{a \times b} = \sqrt{a} \times \sqrt{b}$

and $\quad \sqrt{\dfrac{a}{b}} = \dfrac{\sqrt{a}}{\sqrt{b}}$

Like this

(a) $\sqrt{5} \times \sqrt{20} = \sqrt{5 \times 20} = \sqrt{100} = 10$

(b) $\sqrt{6} \div \sqrt{2} = \dfrac{\sqrt{6}}{\sqrt{2}} = \sqrt{\dfrac{6}{2}} = \sqrt{3}$

Simplifying square roots

You can simplify square roots by writing them as products.

Like this

Simplify $\sqrt{468}$
$468 = 4 \times 9 \times 13$ so you can write
$\sqrt{468} = \sqrt{4 \times 9 \times 13} = \sqrt{4} \times \sqrt{9} \times \sqrt{13} = 2 \times 3 \times \sqrt{13} = 6\sqrt{13}$

Adding and subtracting square roots

This is the same as collecting like terms in algebra. Here the 'like terms' are 'like roots'.

Note: $\sqrt{3}$ is the same as $1\sqrt{3}$

Like this

Simplify: $\sqrt{3} + 5\sqrt{3}$
The like term is $\sqrt{3}$ so $\quad \sqrt{3} + 5\sqrt{3} = 1\sqrt{3} + 5\sqrt{3} = 6\sqrt{3}$

Fractions involving square roots

You will (of course) remember equivalent fractions. To simplify an expression which has a square root in the denominator you multiply the numerator and denominator by the same square root. It is called rationalising.

Like this

Rationalise the denominator of this fraction $\dfrac{2}{\sqrt{5}}$
$$\frac{2}{\sqrt{5}} = \frac{2}{\sqrt{5}} \times \frac{\sqrt{5}}{\sqrt{5}}$$
$$= \frac{2 \times \sqrt{5}}{\sqrt{25}} = \frac{2\sqrt{5}}{5}$$

Practice Exercise

1 Complete this calculation to express $0.\dot{3}4\dot{5}$ as a fraction.

$$1 \times 0.\dot{3}4\dot{5} = 0.345\ 345\ 345\dots$$

$$1000 \times 0.\dot{3}4\dot{5} = \dots\dots\dots\dots\,.\dots\dots\dots$$

$$999 \times 0.\dot{3}4\dot{5} = 345$$

$$\therefore\quad 0.\dot{3}4\dot{5} = \frac{\dots}{\dots} = \frac{\dots}{333}$$

2 Place the following in the correct boxes:

π $\sqrt{2}$ $\sqrt{3}$ $\sqrt{4}$ $\sqrt{2}+1$ π^2

Rational	Irrational

3 Simplify:

(a) $\sqrt{20} + \sqrt{12}$

....

(b) $\sqrt{63} - \sqrt{28}$

....

(c) $\dfrac{\sqrt{50}}{\sqrt{2}}$

....

(d) $\dfrac{\sqrt{27}}{\sqrt{3}}$

....

4 Rationalise these:

(a) $\dfrac{15\sqrt{2}}{\sqrt{5}}$ ....

....

(b) $\dfrac{50}{\sqrt{2}}$ ....

....

(c) $\dfrac{75}{\sqrt{10}}$ ....

....

1. (a) Arrange the following numbers in order of size, smallest first.

   0.085,   0.55,   0.56,   0.555,   0.058,   1,   0

   ....

   (b) Express as decimals

   (i) 54% ....

   (ii) $\frac{4}{5}$ ....

2. Oranges are normally sold in packs of 15 oranges.
   A special offer pack has 20% extra free.
   How many oranges are in the special offer pack?

   ....

   (SEG – specimen paper)

3. In 1990 Elm Tree House was bought for £88 000.

   (a) In 1992 Elm Tree House was sold at a loss of 12.5%.
   What was the sale price?

   ....

   ....

   (b) In 1996 Elm Tree House was sold again. The sale price was 1.5% higher than
   its value in 1990. By how much had the value of the house increased between
   1992 and 1996?

   ....

   ....

   (SEG, Summer 1997 – Paper 3)

4. Bryan buys 21 litres of petrol at 65.9 pence per litre. How much will she be
   charged?

   ....

Examination Questions

5. Which of the following are integers?

$\frac{4}{8}$, $\frac{8}{4}$,   5,   0.5,   56,   5.6

....

6. Arrange the following in order of size, smallest first.

$0.\dot{6}$,   0.7,   0.67,   0.666,   0.6

....

7. A farm has an area of 324 hectares of land.
$\frac{1}{6}$ of the land is woodland and $\frac{5}{18}$ of the land is pasture.
The rest of the land is arable.

(a) What fraction of the land is arable?

....

(b) Calculate the area of the arable land.

....

(NEAB – specimen paper)

8. Skirts were priced at £13.80. In the sale, they cost £12.30.
What percentage discount is this?
Give your answer to an appropriate degree of accuracy.

....

(SEG – specimen paper)

9. In a sale a pair of trainers costs £25. This is a saving of 20%.
What was the original price of the shoes?

....

(NEAB – specimen paper)

10. In a sale a dress costs £32.40. The original price has been reduced by 10%.
What was the original price?

....

(NEAB, Summer 1998 – Intermediate Paper 2I)

Examination Questions

11. $x = 0.\dot{4}\dot{5}$

    (a) Write down the value of $100x$.

    ....

    (b) Work out the value of $99x$.

    ....

    (c) Hence or otherwise, express x in the form $\dfrac{a}{b}$, where a and b are whole numbers.

    ....

    (d) Use a similar method to that above, or otherwise, to express $0.4\dot{5}\dot{6}$ as a rational number.

    ....

    ....

                                    (NEAB – specimen paper)

12. (a) Explain what a rational number is.

    ....

    ....

    (b) Using $(a + b)^2 = a^2 + 2ab + b^2$ or otherwise, show that

$$(\sqrt{2} + \sqrt{8})^2 = 18$$

    You must not use a calculator to answer this question.

    ....

    ....

    (c) Tracey says

> $(\sqrt{2} + \sqrt{8})$ *is an irrational number.*
>
> $(\sqrt{2} + \sqrt{8})^2 = 18$
>
> *I think that if you square an irrational number you always get a rational number!*

    Tracey is wrong. Use an example to show that Tracey is wrong.

    ....

    ....

                                     (NEAB, 1998 – Paper 2H)

13. The number x is given by the formula $x = \sqrt{(a^2 + b^2)}$.

   (a) In each of the following cases, find x and state whether it is a rational or irrational number.

   (i) $a = 5, b = 10$

   ....

   (ii) $a = \sqrt{3}, b = \sqrt{6}$

   ....

   (b) The numbers a and b satisfy

   $$a^2 \leqslant 4, \quad 3 \leqslant b^2 \leqslant 5$$

   Find two pairs of positive numbers, a and b, such that x is rational.

   ....

   ....

   (SEG, 1997 – Higher Paper 6)

14. Simplify the expression $\sqrt{12} \times \sqrt{6}$ leaving your answer in surd form.

   ....

   ....

   (SEG – specimen paper)

15. (a) Which of the following numbers are rational?

   (i) $1 + \sqrt{2}$ ....

   (ii) π^2 ....

   (iii) $3^0 + 3^{-1} + 3^{-2}$ ....

   (b) When p and q are two different irrational numbers, $p \times q$ can be rational. Write down one example to show this.

   ....

   (c) Write down a fraction which is equal to the recurring decimal $0.0\dot{3}\dot{6}$

   ....

   (SEG – specimen paper)

Number

Topic 2
More
number

Note: Compare this
$$\text{with } \frac{6}{14} = \frac{3}{7} = \frac{30}{70}$$

Note: The rest is spent on boring necessities!

Summary

Working with ratios

If two brothers are 3 and 7 years old you can say the ratio of their ages is 3 compared to 7.

You can write 3 compared to 7 (you usually say 3 to 7) as $3:7$.

Writing ratios in different forms

You work with ratios in the same way as you work with fractions.

You do not change a ratio if you multiply or divide both sides of the ratio by the same number.

Like this

$6:14 = 3:7$ (divide by 2) $6:14 = 30:70$ (multiply by 5)

It is sometimes useful to write a ratio in the form $1:n$.

You can write the ratio $3:7$ in the form $1:n$ by dividing both sides by 3.

Like this

$3:7 = 1:\frac{7}{3} = 1:2\frac{1}{3}$

Dividing an amount in a given ratio

You earn £126 and divide it between partying, boring necessities and travel in the ratio $3:7:2$. How much do you spend on partying and how much do you spend on travel?

Rules for dividing an amount in a given ratio

1   Add the numbers in the ratio together. $3 + 7 + 2 = 12$

2   Divide the amount by 12 to get 1 part.

One part is £126 ÷ 12 = £10.50

3   Work out 3 parts and 2 parts.

Partying: Three parts is £10.5 × 3 = £31.50

Travel: Two parts is £10.5 × 2 = £21.00

I spend £31.50 on partying and £21 on travel

Rounding numbers to decimal places

You can round numbers to any number of decimal places.

When rounding numbers, the rule is to look at the next decimal place:

> **if the next decimal place is less than 5 then ignore it**
> **if the next decimal place is 5 or more then round up**

Like this

(a)   Write 3.86 to one decimal place (1 dp).
      To round to 1 decimal place you look at the next (second) decimal place which is 6 so round up.

      $3.86 = 3.9$ (1 dp)

(b)   Write 4.6745 to two decimal places.
      To round to 2 decimal places you look at the next (third) decimal place which is 4 so ignore it.

      $4.6745 = 4.67$ (2 dp)

Practice Exercise

1 Find a set of 6 different positive and negative numbers that add up to zero.

.... + ... + ... + ... + ... + ... = 0

2

Salad dressing
4 parts oil to
1 part vinegar

To make 100 ml of dressing,

you need .... ml oil

and .... ml vinegar.

3 30% of the students in a class are female.

The ratio of males to females is ....

4 Tick one answer.
2.478 rounded to 2 decimal places is

2.4	2.47	2.5	25	0.47
24	24.7	2.48	0.48	48

5 Use your common sense (not your calculator!) to decide which of these statements are reasonable:

✓ or ✗

(a) 53 meals at £4.95 each cost £262.35.   ....

(b) 152 units of electricity at 5.83p per unit cost £1342.16.   ....

(c) 12.3 square metres of carpet at £16.20 per square metre cost £1992.60.   ....

(d) The average of 16.2, 17.9, 27.8 and 15.2 is 77.1.   ....

(e) A salary of £22 531 a year is £1877.58 a week.   ....

Number

Topic 2
More
number

Working with negative numbers

When you multiply or divide two numbers which are either both positive or both negative then the answer is positive.

When you multiply or divide two numbers one positive and the other negative then the answer is negative.

Like this

$$+5 \times +6 = 30 \quad\quad +10 \div +2 = 5 \quad\quad +10 \times -2 = -20 \quad\quad +14 \div -7 = -2$$
$$-3 \times -7 = 21 \quad\quad -12 \div -4 = 3 \quad\quad -3 \times +2 = -6 \quad\quad -12 \div +3 = -4$$

Direct proportion

If two quantities are directly proportional, then as one quantity increases so does the other quantity, keeping the ratio of the quantities the same.

Like this

Find the cost of a railway journey of 105 miles when a railway journey of 20 miles costs £3.20

20 miles costs £3.20

1 mile costs $\dfrac{£3.20}{20}$ $\quad\quad = £0.16$

105 miles costs $105 \times £0.16 = £16.80$

Inverse proportion

If two quantities are inversely proportional, then as one quantity increases the other quantity decreases so that the product remains the same.

Like this

You have provided enough food for 5 happy campers for one week (7 days). It rains and only two campers arrive at the camp.

How long will the food last the 2 campers?

5 campers have food for 7 days

1 camper has food for $7 \times 5 \quad\quad = 35$ days

2 campers have food for $35 \div 2 = 17$ days (and a half day!)

Rounding numbers to significant figures

You can also round numbers to any number of significant figures.

When rounding numbers, the rule is to look at the next significant figure:

> **if the next significant figure is less than 5 then ignore it**
> **if the next significant figure is 5 or more then round up**

Like this

(a) Write 4357 to 3 significant figures.
   The next (fourth) significant figure is 7, so round up.

   $4357 = 4360$ (3 sf)

(b) Write 0.002 718 to 2 significant figures.
   The next (third) significant figure is 1, so ignore it.

   $0.002\,718 = 0.0027$ (2 sf)

Rounding numbers to one significant figure is a useful way of approximating for mental calculations.

Note: Remember that the first significant figure here is 2 as you do not count 0s in front of the number.

Like this

Find an approximate answer for $\quad 62.1 \times 19.8$

Rounding each number to 1 significant figure $\quad 60 \times 20 = 120$

Practice Exercise

1 When the number 3039.673 is rounded to:

	3 significant figures	1 decimal place	nearest whole number	1 significant figure
it becomes:	3000	3	3040	3039.7	3039

Match these up. Which numbers are left over?

....

....

2 Two quantities are inversely proportional.
If one quantity is doubled, what happens to the other?
Illustrate your answer with an example.

....

....

....

....

3 Arrange these in order of size. (Don't use a calculator!)

6.3×10^4 63×100 0.63×10^3 $6.3 \div 10^2$ 0.0063

................., ..., ..., ..., ...

4 Match the questions and the answers:

$0.9 \div -0.3 =$	-30
$-3 \times -9 =$	$+30$
$-9 \div 0.3 =$	-3
$-3 \div 9 =$	$-\frac{1}{3}$
$-9 \div -0.3 =$	$+27$

Number

Topic 2
More
number

Summary

Upper and lower bounds

I know that Chris's height to the nearest whole number is 194 cm.
So Chris's actual height can be anywhere between 193.5 cm and 194.5 cm.
The maximum error in Chris's height is 1 cm ÷ 2 = 0.5 cm.

Like this

(a) Ann's weight is 81.7 kg. Find Ann's smallest and largest weight.

Ann's weight is given to 1 decimal place so the maximum error is
0.1 kg ÷ 2 = 0.05 kg.

Smallest weight is	81.7 kg − 0.05 kg	= 81.65 kg
Largest weight is	81.7 kg + 0.05 kg	= 81.75 kg

Note: *The weight of 81.75 kg would actually be rounded to 81.8 kg but it is easier to write 81.75 than 81.749 999 999 99... (which is very close!).*

(b) Fred's height is 1.62 m. What are the lower and upper limits of Fred's height?

Fred's height is given to 2 decimal places so the maximum error is
0.01 m ÷ 2 = 0.005 m.

Lower limit of Fred's height is	1.62 m − 0.005 m	= 1.615 m
Upper limit of Fred's height is	1.62 m + 0.005 m	= 1.625 m

The effects of approximations on calculations

You take the most extreme value in each case!

Like this

(a) One chocolate bar weighs 65 g to the nearest gram. What is the lowest possible weight of 50 bars?

Weight is given to nearest gram so the maximum error for each bar is
1 g ÷ 2 = 0.5 g.

Lowest weight for 1 chocolate bar is	65 g − 0.5 g	= 64.5 g
Lowest weight for 50 chocolate bars is	50 × 64.5 g	= 3225 g

(b) The length of a rectangle is 3.4 cm and the width is 2.7 cm. What are the lower and upper bounds of the area?

Note: *Give the answer to a reasonable degree of accuracy, remembering that the original measurements were only given to 1 decimal place.*

Measurements are given to 1 decimal place so the maximum error is
0.1 cm ÷ 2 = 0.05 cm.

Lowest length is 3.35 cm and lowest width is 2.65 cm.

So lowest area is	3.35 × 2.65 cm^2	= 8.8775 cm^2

Greatest length is 3.45 cm and greatest width is 2.75 cm.

So biggest area is	3.45 × 2.75 cm^2	= 9.4875 cm^2

The area lies between 8.9 cm^2 and 9.5 cm^2 (rounded to 1 dp).

Practice Exercise

1 (a) Match the statements. If a length x metres is given as 3 metres then:

correct to the nearest metre	$2.95 \leqslant x < 3.05$
correct to the nearest cm	$2.5 \leqslant x < 3.5$
correct to the nearest 10 cm	$2.995 \leqslant x < 3.005$

(b) What are the upper and lower bounds if x is given as 3 m correct to the nearest 5 cm?

....

....

....

2 The weights of 4 suitcases correct to the nearest kilogram are given as

19 kg,   21 kg,   13 kg   and   17 kg

Would it be safe to put them all on a trolley that can take a maximum weight of 70 kg?

Explain your answer.

....

....

....

....

....

....

Number

Topic 2
More
number

1. (a) Arrange these numbers in order of size, smallest first.

$$0, \quad -5, \quad 2, \quad -8, \quad 4, \quad -2, \quad -1$$

....

(b) Find the sum of the numbers in part (a).

....

2. In a class there are 12 boys and 16 girls.

(a) Find the boy : girl ratio in its simplest form.

....

(b) What percentage of the class are boys?

....

3. A town has a population of 645 166 people.
The ratio of retired people to the rest of the population is 1 : 3.
How many people are retired?
Give your answer correct to three significant figures.

....

(SEG, Summer 1998 – Paper 13)

4. 80 million pounds of lottery funds was given to the sports of swimming and athletics. This money was shared between these two sports in the ratio

swimming : athletics
3 : 1

Calculate the amount that was given to swimming.

....

....

(NEAB, 1998 – Intermediate Paper 1I)

5. Anne drives 559 miles using 53.7 litres of diesel. Calculate how far she goes on one litre of diesel, giving your answer to an appropriate degree of accuracy.

....

6. Evaluate $5 \times (-6) + (-10)$

   ....

7. A petrol pump takes 20 seconds to fill an 8 litre can. How long will it take to fill a 70 litre car fuel tank?

   ....

   ....

8. (a) Work out $\dfrac{4.7 \times 20.1}{5.6 - 1.8}$. Write down your full calculator display.

   ....

   (b) Use estimation to check your answer.

   ....

   (NEAB, Summer 1998 – Paper 2I)

9. In 1995 Mr Royles drove 7764 miles in his car. His car does 37 miles per gallon. Petrol costs 52 pence per litre.

   (a) By taking one gallon to be 4.55 litres, calculate, in £, how much Mr Royles spent on petrol in 1995.

   ....

   ....

   (b) Show how you can use approximation to check that your answer is of the right order of magnitude. You **must** show all your working.

   ....

   ....

   (SEG – specimen paper)

Number

Topic 2
More
number

Examination Questions

10. (a) Mr Grey receives an electricity bill for £42.91. The bill includes a quarterly charge of £10.33 and the cost per unit is 7.49 pence. Mr Grey writes down the following calculation to work out the number of units of electricity he has used.

$$\text{Units used} = \frac{(42.91 - 10.33) \times 100}{7.49}$$

Calculate, to the nearest whole number, how many units he has used.

....

....

(b) In the next quarter he uses 578 units. The quarterly charge is the same and the cost per unit is the same. Calculate this quarterly bill.

....

....

(SEG – specimen paper)

11. Jean is told to estimate the value of $876 \div 32$. She says it is about 30. Explain how you could do this by estimation.

....

....

....

(NEAB – specimen paper)

12. Complete the following:

(a) $-4 - \text{............} = -9$

(b) $6 - \text{............} = 8$

(NEAB, Winter '98 – Intermediate Paper 1I)

13. In 1954, Roger Bannister ran a mile in a time of 239.2 seconds, correct to the nearest tenth of a second. What is the shortest time that it could actually be?

....

(SEG – specimen paper)

Examination Questions

Number

**Topic 2
More
number**

Higher Tier Only

14. Mr Jones weighs his case on his bathroom scales, which weigh to the nearest kilogram. He finds that his case weighs 20 kg.

   (a) What are the greatest and least weights of the case?

   ....

   ....

   (b) On the way to the airport he removes a sweater from his case. At the airport the scale gives the weight of his case as 19.4 kg to the nearest tenth of a kilogram. What is the heaviest weight that the sweater could be?

   ....

   ....

   ....

   (NEAB, Summer 1998 – Higher Paper 2H)

15. Sections of a railway line are measured to the nearest metre as either 200 m or 80 m. What are the upper and lower bounds on the total length of 15 sections consisting of eight 200 m sections and seven 80 m sections?

   ....

   ....

   ....

   (SEG – specimen paper)

16. (a) The sides of a rectangle have dimensions 20 cm and 30 cm each measured to the nearest centimetre. Calculate the smallest possible area of the rectangle.

   ....

   ....

   ....

   (b) The sides of a square have length x cm measured to the nearest centimetre. Write down and simplify an expression, in terms of x, for the difference between the largest and smallest possible areas of the square.

   ....

   ....

   ....

   ....

   (SEG, Summer 1998 – Higher Paper 15)

Topic 3
Describing number

*Note: 1 is **not** a prime number (because it only has one factor).*

Summary

Prime numbers

A **prime number** is a number which has only 2 factors (1 and itself).
So the prime numbers are 2, 3, 5, 7, 11, 13, 17, 19, 23, 29, 31, ...

All numbers can be expressed as products of prime numbers.

Like this

Find the prime factors of 2100.

You must divide 2100 by the smallest prime number (2) until it will divide no more!

$$2100 \div 2 = 1050$$
$$1050 \div 2 = 525$$

Now try to divide by the next smallest prime number (3): $525 \div 3 = 175$

Now try to divide by the next smallest prime number (5): $175 \div 5 = 35$
$$35 \div 5 = 7$$

Now try to divide by the next smallest prime number (7): $7 \div 7 = 1$

As you cannot divide any further then the prime factors of 2100 are 2, 2, 3, 5, 5 and 7 and $2100 = 2 \times 2 \times 3 \times 5 \times 5 \times 7$

Working with standard form

Standard form is a way to write very large numbers such as those used in space exploration, or very small numbers such as those used when dealing with molecules.

First be certain that you are happy multiplying and dividing by powers of 10 without using your calculator.

Like this

(a) To multiply by 10^2 move the decimal point two places to the right.
$$4567.0 \times 10^2 = 456\,700$$

(b) To divide by 10^4 move the decimal point four places to the left.
$$4567.0 \div 10^4 = 0.4567$$

Note:
+ for a large number,
− for a small number.

Rules for writing a number in standard form

1 Write the number so that it is greater than 1 but less than 10.
2 Count the number of decimal places moved.
3 Multiply the new number by $10^{\pm \text{ the number of places moved}}$

Like this

(a) Write 135.0 in standard form.
   1 Write the number as 1.35
   2 So move decimal point 2 places to the left.
   3 Multiply 1.35 by 10^2.
   In standard form $135.0 = 1.35 \times 10^2$

Note:
You can also use your calculator for numbers in standard form.
You use the [EXP] *key or the* [EE] *key on your calculator – but remember to interpret the display properly.*

(b) Write these numbers in standard form:
   (i) 24 609.3
       $= 2.460\,93 \times 10^4$ move the decimal point 4 places left
   (ii) 0.07
       $= 7.0 \times 10^{-2}$ move the decimal point 2 places right
   (iii) 50 million
       $= 50\,000\,000$
       $= 5.0 \times 10^7$ move the decimal point 7 places left

Practice Exercise

1 Which of these are correct?

45 million in standard form is

(a) 45×10^6

(b) 4.5×10^7

(c) 4.5^6

(d) 4.5^7

(e) 45 000 000

Note: There is only one right answer!

1 Answer ....

2 Complete this process to express 240 as a product of prime factors.

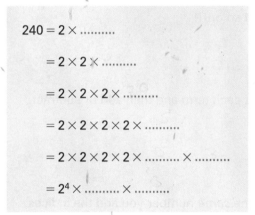

$240 = 2 \times$ ....

$= 2 \times 2 \times$ ....

$= 2 \times 2 \times 2 \times$ ....

$= 2 \times 2 \times 2 \times 2 \times$ ....

$= 2 \times 2 \times 2 \times 2 \times$ .... $\times$ ....

$= 2^4 \times$ .... $\times$ ....

3 Draw lines to match up the pairs of equal numbers.

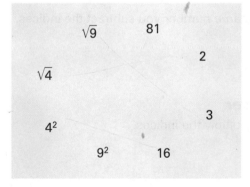

$\sqrt{9}$ 81

2

$\sqrt{4}$

3

4^2

9^2 16

4 Write these standard form numbers out in full.

(a) 4.32×10^5 (b) 2.06×10^2 (c) 8.15×10^{-3}

....

....

....

Number

Topic 3 Describing number

Summary

A little about square and cube roots

Square root $\sqrt{}$

$\sqrt{25} = 5$ You say the square root of 25 is 5 (since $25 = 5 \times 5$)

Cube root $\sqrt[3]{}$

$\sqrt[3]{8} = 2$ You say the cube root of 8 is 2 (since $8 = 2 \times 2 \times 2$)

Powers or indices

Positive indices

2^5 means $2 \times 2 \times 2 \times 2 \times 2 = 32$ You say two to the power of five.

Zero index

Any number to the power of 0 is 1.

Note: You can work out powers on your calculator by using the $\boxed{x^y}$ or $\boxed{y^x}$ button.

Like this

$7^0 = 1$ $10\,000\,002^0 = 1$ and so on!!!

The rules of indices

Adding and subtracting indices

You have to slog it out: work out each term and then add or subtract.

Like this

$2^4 + 2^3 = 16 + 8 = 24$
$2^4 - 2^3 = 16 - 8 = 8$

Multiplying indices

To multiply different powers of the *same* number you add the indices.

Note:
$2^2 \times 2^3 = 4 \times 8 = 32$

Like this

$2^2 \times 2^3 = 2^{2+3} = 2^5$

Dividing indices

To divide different powers of the *same* number you subtract the indices.

Note:
$2^2 \div 2^3 = 4 \div 8 = \frac{1}{2}$

Like this

$2^2 \div 2^3 = 2^{2-3} = 2^{-1}$

Raising powers to a power

To raise powers to a power you multiply the indices.

Like this

$(5^3)^2 = 5^{3 \times 2} = 5^6 = 15\,625$

Reciprocal

To find the reciprocal of a number you turn it upside down (simple!).

Note: You cannot find the reciprocal of 0.

Like this

The reciprocal of $\frac{3}{5}$ is $\frac{5}{3}$

The reciprocal of 3 is $\frac{1}{3}$ you need to write 3 as $\frac{3}{1}$

Practice Exercise

1 Put these terms into circles with others which are equivalent

$$ab \times ab \qquad\qquad bab \qquad\qquad ba^2$$

$$\sqrt{a^2b^2} \qquad\qquad \sqrt{a^4b^4} \qquad\qquad b^2a \qquad\qquad (ab)^2$$

$$\frac{a^2}{a} \times \frac{b^2}{b} \qquad\qquad \frac{a^3b^3}{ab} \qquad\qquad a \times a \times b \qquad\qquad \frac{(ab)^2}{ab}$$

$$ab^2 \qquad\qquad a^2b^2 \qquad\qquad a^2b \qquad\qquad ab$$

2 Arrange these in order of size, starting with the smallest.

4.8×10^{-3} 2.4 2.4×10^{-3} 0.48

0.000 48   240 2.4×10^3 4.8×10^2

....

....

3 Link the reciprocal pairs.

2	$\frac{2}{9}$
4	0.5
$3\frac{1}{3}$	$\frac{1}{4}$
100	0.01
$4\frac{1}{2}$	$\frac{3}{10}$

4 Complete the following:

(a) The highest common factor (HCF) of two numbers is

....

(b) The lowest common multiple (LCM) of two numbers is

....

Topic 3 Describing number

Note: The reciprocal of $\frac{3}{4}$ is $\frac{4}{3}$ and the reciprocal of 8 is $\frac{1}{8}$ (as 8 can be written $\frac{8}{1}$).

Note: You can either use your brain or else the appropriate button on your calculator. The calculator displays the answer: 0.015 625.

Note: To work out the roots of more difficult numbers you use $\boxed{x^{1/y}}$ key on your calculator.

Note: Using you calculator gives you an answer of 0.037 037 0... and you now have the joy of converting your calculator answer to a fraction! 'Brains is best!'

Summary

Negative indices

A negative index always turns the function upside down, that is, gives the **reciprocal**.

$5^{-1} = \frac{1}{5}$　　the index -1 turns the number upside down

$10^{-4} = \frac{1}{10^4} = \frac{1}{10\,000}$　　the index -4 turns the number upside down and raises it to the power of 4

Like this

Work out: 4^{-3}.

$4^{-3} = \frac{1}{4^3} = \frac{1}{64}$

Fractional indices

Fractional indices give the roots of a number.

Like this

$4^{\frac{1}{2}} \times 4^{\frac{1}{2}} = 4^1 = 4$

So $4^{\frac{1}{2}}$ means the square root of 4.

$4^{\frac{1}{2}} = \sqrt{4} = 2$

Similarly $64^{\frac{1}{3}}$ means the cube root of 64

$64^{\frac{1}{3}} = \sqrt[3]{64} = 4$

The rules of indices apply to fractional indices

Like this

Work out $9^{-\frac{3}{2}}$ giving your answer as a fraction.

Using your brains

$9^{-\frac{3}{2}}$　$\frac{1}{9^{\frac{3}{2}}}$　the negative index gives the reciprocal raising the index to a power $9^{\frac{1}{2}}$ is the square root of 9

$= \frac{1}{(9^{\frac{1}{2}})^3}$

$= \frac{1}{3^3}$

$= \frac{1}{27}$

Practice Exercise

1 Match each expression with an equivalent one.

$\sqrt[3]{a}$	$b^{\frac{1}{2}}$
$\sqrt{b}$	a^{-2}
$a^3\sqrt{a}$	$a^{\frac{1}{2}}b^{\frac{1}{2}}$
$\sqrt{ab}$	$a^{3.5}$
$\dfrac{1}{a^2}$	$a^{\frac{1}{3}}$
$\dfrac{1}{\sqrt{b}}$	$b^{-\frac{1}{2}}$

2 Without using a calculator, evaluate these

(a) $64^{\frac{3}{2}}$

(b) $\left(\dfrac{1}{2}\right)^{-2}$

(c) $\left(\dfrac{1}{4}\right)^{-\frac{1}{2}}$

(d) $\sqrt[4]{81}$

Topic 3
Describing number

Examination Questions

1. A light year is the distance travelled by light in 365 days. The speed of light is 3.0×10^5 kilometres per second. The distance to the nearest star is 4.0×10^{13} km. How many light years is it to the nearest star? Give your answer to an appropriate degree of accuracy.

   ....

   ....

   ....

   ....

   ....

   (SEG – specimen paper)

2. Tony used his calculator and from the display he thought that the answer was 4.5^{10}.
   William said that this was the number 45.
   Susan said it was 4.500 000 000 0.
   Joseph said that it was 45 000 000 000.
   Who was correct?

   ....

   (NEAB – specimen paper)

3. Which of these numbers have exact square roots?

   4,   8,   12,   16,   20,   24

   ....

4. (a) Work out the value of 2^5.

   ....

   ....

   (b) A pupil worked out 5^2 instead of 2^5. Calculate the difference between the two answers.

   ....

   ....

   (NEAB – specimen paper)

5. Calculate the difference between $\sqrt{5}$ and $\sqrt[3]{10}$. Give your answer correct to two decimal places.

....

....

(NEAB – specimen paper)

6. 500 sheets of paper make a pile 5 cm high. Express the thickness of one sheet of paper in cm in standard form.

....

....

7. Express these in the form 3^n

(a) $3^2 \times 3^5$ ....

(b) $\dfrac{3^6}{3^2}$ ....

8. (a) Find, as a single integer, the highest common factor of 216 and 168.

....

....

(b) A rectangular field measures 21.6 m by 16.8 m. Fencing posts are placed along its sides at equal distances apart so that fence panels of equal size can be fastened between them. The posts are as far apart as possible. What is the distance between them?

....

....

(SEG – specimen paper)

9. Which is bigger, the square root of 200 or the cube root of 2000? Show how you obtained your answer.

....

....

Topic 3
Describing
number

Examination Questions

10. (a) In Britain there are 5.80×10^7 people.
The number of retired people is 1.04×10^7.
What percentage of people in Britain are retired?
Give your answer to an appropriate degree of accuracy.

....

....

....

(b) 13.8% of the world's population live in Europe.
The population of the world is 5.72×10^9.
Calculate the population of Europe.

....

....

....

(SEG, Summer 1998 – Higher Paper 15)

11. The distance from Earth to the planet Kronos is 35 000 000 000 000 000 miles.
(a) Write this distance in standard form.

....

(b) Light travels at a speed of 5.9×10^{12} miles per year. How many years will it
take to travel from Kronos to Earth? Give your answer to a reasonable degree
of accuracy.

....

....

....

....

(NEAB, specimen paper)

12. (a) Find the values of x, y and z in the following equations

    (i) $3^x = 81$

    (ii) $5^y = \dfrac{1}{25}$

    (iii) $1000^z = 10$

....

....

(b) Express $\sqrt{32}$ in the form 2^r.

....

....

(NEAB – specimen paper)

13. Do not use a calculator for this question. Show all your working.

    (a) Simplify $\dfrac{a^6 c^4}{a^2 c^5}$

....

....

(b) Evaluate

    (i) 4^{-2}

....

....

    (ii) $(8)^{1/3}$

....

....

(NEAB, Winter 1998 – Paper 2H)

14. $\dfrac{1}{\sqrt{12}}$ can be written in the form $2^{-1} \times 3^x$. Find the value of x.

....

....

(SEG, Summer 1998 – Higher Paper 16)

Topic 4
Application of number

Note: The amount of taxable income is found by subtracting the personal allowance from the annual income.

Note: The exchange rates fluctuate on a day-to-day basis so examination questions will provide you with the information needed.

Taxation at basic rate

Income tax is a tax on income earned which is paid to the government and is usually deducted automatically from a person's pay packet. The amount of income tax paid depends upon a number of factors such as the amount of money earned, the rate of tax and an individual's personal allowance.

Like this

A shopworker earns £545.60 per month. He has a personal allowance of £3765 and pays 20% on the first £3900 of his taxable income. How much income tax does he pay?

Annual income is £545.60 × 12 = £6547.20
Taxable income is annual income − personal allowance
= £6547.20 − £3765.00 = £2782.20

The shopworker pays 20% tax on the first £3900 of his taxable income.

$$\text{Tax} = 20\% \text{ of } £2782.20 = \frac{20}{100} \times £2782.20 = £556.44$$

The shopworker pays £556.44 income tax.

Foreign currency and exchange rates

The table gives the exchange rate for the British pound at the time of going to press.

You will be expected to answer questions on foreign currency and exchange rates.

Country	Exchange rate
Australia	£1 = 2.62 dollars
Austria	£1 = 18.94 schillings
Belgium	£1 = 55.73 francs
Denmark	£1 = 10.33 kroner
France	£1 = 9.03 francs
Germany	£1 = 2.70 marks
Greece	£1 = 453.55 dracma
Holland	£1 = 3.03 guilders
Ireland	£1 = 1.08 punts
Italy	£1 = 2688.00 lira
Japan	£1 = 193.88 yen
New Zealand	£1 = 3.10 dollars
Spain	£1 = 228.60 pesetas
Sweden	£1 = 13.17 kroner
United States	£1 = 1.61 dollars

Like this

(a) How many Swedish kroner would you get for £120?

The exchange rate is £1 = 13.17 kroner.
So £120 = 120 × 13.17 kroner
= 1580 kroner (to the nearest kroner)

(b) How much is 150 French francs worth?

The exchange rate is 9.03 francs = £1

$$1 \text{ franc} = \frac{£1}{9.03} \qquad (\div 9.03 \text{ to find the value of 1 franc})$$

$$150 \text{ francs} = 150 \times \frac{£1}{9.03} \qquad (\times 150 \text{ to find the value of 150 francs})$$

$$= £16.61 \qquad (\text{to the nearest penny})$$

Working with simple interest

With simple interest you only get interest paid on the amount you originally invested (not very interesting at all).

Like this

A bank account gives 9.325% simple interest per annum (each year). Find out how much interest you earn on £3000 invested for 4 years.

$$1\text{st year's interest is } 9.325\% \text{ of } £3000 = \frac{9.325}{100} \times £3000 = £279.75$$

4 years' interest is £279.75 × 4 = £1119.00

Practice Exercise

1 Compare the prices of different sizes of shampoo:

Small size: 100 ml for £1.29 so 1 ml costs ....

Large size: 250 ml for £3.10 so 1 ml costs ....

Best buy is ....

Check your answer:

Small size: 100 ml for £1.29 so 1 penny buys ....

Large size: 250 ml for £3.10 so 1 penny buys ....

Best buy is ....

2 Mike chooses clothes costing £57.45 but he gets a 5% student discount. How much will he pay?

$$\text{Discount} = \frac{.............}{100} \times £57.45 = ...$$

$$\text{Price paid} = £57.45 - £..................... = £.....................$$

3 Which of these calculations will give the correct answer for $\dfrac{3.2 + 21.9}{5.6}$?

(a) $3.2 + 21.9 \div 5.6$

(b) $(3.2 + 21.9) \div 5.6$

(c) $3.2 + (21.9 \div 5.6)$

(d) $5.6 \div (3.2 + 21.9)$

3 Answer ....

Number

Topic 4
Application of number

Note: Remember that **per** *tells you to divide.*

Note: For problems involving compound measure (that is **per***!) keep your wits about you and make sure you know when to divide and when to multiply.*

Summary

Working with compound interest

With compound interest you get interest paid on your interest. To calculate compound interest you find the interest for the first year. You then add this interest to the original amount and find the interest on this new amount for the second year. And so on!

Like this

Find the compound interest on £200 invested for 3 years at 10% per annum.

10% as a decimal is 0.1	1st year interest is $0.1 \times £200 = £20$
New amount is £200 + £20 = £220	2nd year interest is $0.1 \times £220 = £22$
New amount is £220 + £22 = £242	3rd year interest is $0.1 \times £242 = £24.20$

For 3 years the total interest is £20 + £22 + £24.20 = £66.20

Working with compound measure

Examples of compound measure are:

> speed measured in miles per hour
> density measured in grams per cubic centimetre
> population density measured in people per square mile.

For a problem involving speed you may find it helps to use a **D**istance, **S**peed, **T**ime triangle.

$$\text{Distance} = \text{Speed} \times \text{Time}$$

$$\text{Speed} = \frac{\text{Distance}}{\text{Time}} \qquad \text{Time} = \frac{\text{Distance}}{\text{Speed}}$$

Like this

A car travels at 35 mph for 2 hours. It stops for 30 minutes, and then continues at a steady speed of 70 mph along the motorway for 3 hours 45 minutes. Find the car's average speed over the whole journey.

$$\text{Average speed} = \frac{\text{Total distance}}{\text{Total time}}$$

Total time is 2 h + 0.5 h + 3.75 h	= 6.25 h
Distance for first part of journey is 35 mph × 2 h	= 70 miles
Distance for second part of journey is 70 mph × 3.75 h	= 262.5 miles
Total distance is 70 miles + 262.5 miles	= 332.5 miles

$$\text{Average speed} = \frac{332.5}{6.25}\text{ mph} = 53.2\text{ mph}$$

Similarly, for a problem involving density you may find it helps to use a **M**ass, **D**ensity, **V**olume triangle.

$$\text{Mass} = \text{Density} \times \text{Volume}$$

$$\text{Density} = \frac{\text{Mass}}{\text{Volume}} \qquad \text{Volume} = \frac{\text{Mass}}{\text{Density}}$$

Practice Exercise

1 Tax is paid at 20% per annum on the first £3900 of taxable income and at 23% on the remaining taxable income up to £27 000.

Find the tax paid by a person with £16 500 taxable income.

....

....

....

1 Answer £.........................

2 Explain how to find the mass of a cuboid whose measurements are given (in cm) and which is made of material with a density of 3 grams per cubic centimetre.

....

....

....

3 Complete these calculations to give the total amount after 2 years if £100 is invested at 3% per annum interest.

Interest for 1st year = $\dfrac{3}{100}$ × £100 = ...

Amount at beginning of 2nd year = £100 + ... = ...

Interest for 2nd year = $\dfrac{..........}{..........}$ × £.................. = ...

∴ Amount at end of 2nd year = ...

4 (a) Calculate £100 × (1.03)².

....

....

(b) Compare your answer with that for question 3 and comment.

....

....

....

Topic 4
Application of number

Note: '∝' means 'is proportional to'. k is called the constant of proportionality.

Summary

Proportion and inverse proportion

1 If you are told you can write
or

y is (directly) proportional to x
$y \propto x$
$y = kx$

2 Similarly if you can write
or

y is (directly) proportional to $\sqrt{x}$
$y \propto \sqrt{x}$
$y = k\sqrt{x}$

3 If you are told you can write

or

y is inversely proportional to x
$y \propto \dfrac{1}{x}$
$y = k \times \dfrac{1}{x}$ that is $yx = k$

4 Similarly, if you can write

or

y is inversely proportional to x^2
$y \propto \dfrac{1}{x^2}$
$y = k \times \dfrac{1}{x^2}$ that is $yx^2 = k$

Exam questions usually require you to write the appropriate formula and give you some information to calculate k.

Like this

The weight (w grams) of a sphere is directly proportional to the radius (r centimetres) cubed. When the radius is 2 cm the weight is 4 g. Find the weight of a sphere made of the same material having a radius of 5 cm.

The proportion formula is: $w = kr^3$

Substitute $r = 2$, $w = 4$ $4 = k \times 2^3$
                                                    $4 = 8k$

so $k = 4 \div 8 = 0.5$

The formula is: $w = 0.5r^3$

When $r = 5$ $w = 0.5 \times 5^3 = 62.5$

So the weight of the sphere is 62.5 g

Practice Exercise

1 Decide whether each pair of variables is directly proportional, inversely proportional, or neither.

(a) Length and width of a rectangle with fixed perimeter.

1a Answer ....

(b) Length and width of a rectangle with fixed area.

1b Answer ....

(c) Time taken and distance travelled at constant speed.

1c Answer ....

(d) Speed and time taken for journey of fixed distance.

1d Answer ....

(e) Length and perimeter of square.

1e Answer ....

(f) Length and area of square.

1f Answer ....

2 Link the following:

y varies inversely as x	$y \propto x^{-3}$
y is proportional to x	$y \propto x^3$
y is inversely proportional to the square root of x	$y \propto \dfrac{1}{\sqrt{x}}$
y is proportional to the cube root of x	$y \propto x$
y varies as the cube of x	$y \propto \dfrac{1}{x}$
y is inversely proportional to x cubed	$y \propto x^{\frac{1}{3}}$

3 P varies directly as the square root of Q.
If $P = 6$ when $Q = 100$ find the value of P when $Q = 64$

Topic 4
Application of number

Examination Questions

1. A man wants to exchange £450 for Singapore Dollars. The exchange rate is 3.4 Singapore Dollars for £1.

   (a) How many Singapore Dollars are equivalent to £450?

   ....

   (b) The man buys a watch which costs 27 Singapore Dollars. What is this worth in £? Give your answer to the nearest £.

   ....

   ....

   (NEAB – specimen paper)

2. The size and selling price of small and medium toothpaste are shown.

Small size 72 ml **50p**	Medium size 135 ml **90p**

   Which size of toothpaste gives better value for money? You **must** show all your working.

   ....

   ....

   ....

   (SEG – specimen paper)

3. Given that y is proportional to x^2, complete the table.

x	5		20
y	45	180	

   (SEG, Summer '98 – Higher Paper 15)

4. A car travels at 28 metres per second.
   What is its speed in kilometres per hour? Give your answer to an appropriate degree of accuracy.

   ....

   ....

   ....

   (SEG, Summer '97 – Higher Paper 5)

Examination Questions

5. Kathy earned £27 000 in 1995. She did not pay tax on the first £3525 of her income. She paid tax on the rest of her income at the following tax rates. She paid tax at 20% on the first £3200 of her taxable income and at 25% on the rest of her taxable income. Calculate the total amount of tax that she paid in 1995.

   ....

   ....

   ....

   ....

   (SEG – specimen paper)

6. (a) A train from London to Manchester takes 2 hours 30 minutes. It travels at an average speed of 80 miles an hour.
       What is the distance from London to Manchester?

   ....

   ....

   (b) The railway company is going to buy some faster trains. These new trains will have an average speed of 100 miles per hour.
       How much time will be saved on the journey from London to Manchester?

   ....

   ....

   ....

   (NEAB, Summer 1998 – Intermediate Paper 1I)

7. The formula for the population, P, of a country with a growth rate of $r\%$ per year in time t years, is given by $P = P_0\left(1 + \dfrac{r}{100}\right)^t$ where P_0 is the population this year. The population of Nigeria this year is 66.2 million. The growth rate is 3% per year. Calculate the population of Nigeria in five years time giving your answer to an appropriate degree of accuracy.

   ....

   ....

   ....

   ....

   (SEG – specimen paper)

8. A cuboid measures 5 cm by 5 cm by 10 cm. Its mass is 0.354 kg. Calculate the density of the cuboid in grams per cubic centimetre.

   ....

   ....

   ....

Examination Questions

9. The wavelength, w metres, of radio waves is inversely proportional to the frequency, f kHz, of the waves.

   (a) A radio wavelength of 1000 metres has a frequency of 300 kHz. The frequency is doubled to 600 kHz. What is the new wavelength?

   ....

   ....

   (b) Calculate the frequency when the wavelength is 842 metres.

   ....

   ....

   (c) Radio NEAB has a frequency in kHz which is numerically equal to its wavelength in metres.
   Calculate the wavelength of Radio NEAB.

   ....

   ....

   (NEAB, Summer 1998 – Higher Paper 1H)

10. The number, N, of square tiles needed to tile a floor varies inversely as the square of the length, L m, of the side of the tile.
    When $L = 0.4$, $N = 2000$

    (a) Find a formula connecting N and L

    ....

    ....

    (b) Calculate the number of tiles when $L = 0.6$.

    ....

    ....

    (SEG – specimen paper)

Examination Questions

11. The value, £v, of a car is inversely proportional to its age, y years.

After 2 years the car has a value of £3500.

Use this information to find

(a) the value of the car after 5 years

....

....

....

....

(b) the age of the car when it is worth £1000

....

....

....

....

12. A car travels at an average speed of 30 miles per hour. How long will it take to do a journey of 100 miles? Give your answer in hours and minutes..

....

....

(NEAB – specimen paper)

13. A solid plastic cuboid has dimensions 3 cm by 5 cm by 9 cm. The density of the plastic is 0.95 grams per cm³. What is the weight of this plastic cuboid?

....

....

(NEAB, Winter '98 – Paper 1I)

Algebra

Topic 5
The language of algebra

Note: ab *and* 4ba *are like terms as* ab *is the same as* ba.

Note: The number in front of a term is sometimes called the coefficient. For 6xy the coefficient of xy is 6.

Note:
$-(2x + 4) = -2x - 4$
as you multiply each term inside the bracket by -1 (-1 times 2x plus -1 times 4).

Note: Always check you have the correct answer by multiplying out.

Summary

Simplifying expressions

Addition and subtraction

You can only add and subtract like terms.

Like this

(a) $y + 2y = 3y$ (add like y terms)

(b) $y^2 - 3y^2 = -2y^2$ (subtract like y^2 terms)

(c) $ab + 4ba = 5ab$ or $5ba$ (as $ab = ba$)

(d) $3y^2 + 2y^3$ (you cannot add these because y^3 and y^2 are unlike terms)

Multiplication

To multiply two terms you multiply the numbers then the letters.

Like this

(a) $5y \times 7y = 5 \times 7 \times y \times y = 35y^2$

(b) $2ab \times 6bc = 2 \times 6 \times a \times b \times b \times c = 12ab^2c$

Division

To divide two terms you should cancel down where possible.

Like this

(a) $6xy \div 6y = \dfrac{^3\cancel{6}x\cancel{y}}{_1\cancel{2}\cancel{y}} = 3x$

(b) $4p^2qr^3 \div 3pq^2r^2 = \dfrac{4p^2qr^3}{3pq^2r^2} = \dfrac{4pr}{3q}$

Working with brackets

Expanding brackets

If there is a term outside the bracket then it must multiply every term inside the bracket. This process is called expanding the brackets.

Like this

(a) Expand $3(y + 4)$.

   $3(y + 4) = 3y + 12$ (you multiply each term inside the bracket by 3, i.e. 3 times y plus 3 times 4)

(b) Expand $-4y(y + 5)$.

   $-4y(y + 5) = -4y^2 - 20y$ (you multiply each term inside the bracket by $-4y$, i.e. $-4y$ times y plus $-4y$ times 5)

Factorising brackets

The opposite of expanding brackets is factorising brackets. Factorising means putting the brackets back by looking for common factors.

Like this

(a) Factorise $3x + 6$
   $3x + 6 = 3 \times x + 3 \times 2$
   $\qquad\quad = 3(x + 2)$ (3 is the common factor)

(b) Factorise $y^2 + 4y$
   $y^2 + 4y = y \times y + 4 \times y$
   $\qquad\quad = y(y + 4)$ (y is the common factor)

Practice Exercise

1 Use different colours to shade the boxes containing like terms.

Note: You should only need 4 different colours.

x	$2y$	z	xy
$7y$	$4z$	$3x$	xyx
$2xyz$	$5x$	$\frac{1}{2}zyx$	$-\frac{1}{2}y$
$3xy$	$\frac{1}{3}y$	$-yx$	$-2x$

2 Circle the correct answer(s).

(a) $y + 5y =$ $\quad y + 5y \qquad y + 6 \qquad 6y$

(b) $ab + ba =$ $\quad ba + ab \qquad 2ab \qquad abba$

(c) $ab \times ab =$ $\quad abab \qquad 2ab \qquad a^2b^2$

(d) $6xy \div 2y =$ $\quad 12xy^2 \qquad 6x \qquad 3x$

(e) $4(x + 2) =$ $\quad 4x + 2 \qquad 4x + 8 \qquad 4x + 42$

(f) $y(y - 3) =$ $\quad yy - 3 \qquad y - 3y \qquad y^2 - 3y$

3 Find the trios of equivalent expressions. One set has been done for you.

$3(x - 6)$	$18 - 3x$	$-3(-6 + x)$
$3(6 - x)$	$3x + 18$	$-3(x + 6)$
$3(x + 6)$	$-3x - 18$	$-3(-x - 6)$
$3(-x - 6)$	$3x - 18$	$-3(-x + 6)$

4 Think of a number.
Double it. Add 6.
Divide the answer by 2.
Take away the number you first thought of.
What number do you have now?

Show why the result will **always** be 3 no matter what number you start with.

....

....

5 Which of these expressions is the odd one out?

$abab \quad b^2a^2 \quad (ab)^2 \quad aabb \quad ab^2 \quad baba \quad a^2b^2 \quad (ba)^2$

5 Answer ...... ab^2 ......

Topic 5
The language of algebra

Summary

More working with brackets

Expanding two pairs of brackets

If there are two pairs of brackets then you must multiply each term in the first bracket by each term in the second bracket.

The word **FOIL** (standing for **First, Outside, Inside, Last**) will help you to remember how to do this.

Like this

Expand and simplify $(2x + 3)(x - 4)$

First	$2x \times x = 2x^2$	$(2x + 3)(x - 4)$
Outside	$2x \times -4 = -8x$	$(2x + 3)(x - 4)$
Inside	$3 \times x = 3x$	$(2x + 3)(x - 4)$
Last	$3 \times -4 = -12$	$(2x + 3)(x - 4)$

$$= 2x^2 - 5x - 12 \quad \text{(collecting together like terms)}$$

Factorising quadratics

To factorise quadratics of the form $x^2 + bx + c$ you must look for factors of the number term whose sum is the coefficient of the x term.

Like this

(a) Factorise $x^2 + 7x + 10$
Ask yourself which two numbers multiple to give $+10$ and add to make $+7$.
The numbers are **+2** and **+5**.
So $x^2 + 7x + 10 = (x + 2)(x + 5)$

(b) Factorise $x^2 + 1x - 6$
Ask yourself which two numbers multiply to give -6 and add to make $+1$.
The numbers are **−2** and **+3**.
So $x^2 + 1x - 6 = (x - 2)(x + 3)$

The rules of indices

These are the same as for numbers (see Topic 3).

Multiplying indices

To multiply powers of the *same* letter you add the indices.

Note: You cannot simplify $a^4 + a^5$ or $a^4 - a^5$ because you have unlike terms.

Like this
$$a^4 \times a^5 = a^{4+5} = a^9$$

Dividing indices

To divide powers of the *same* letter you subtract the indices.

Like this
$$a^4 \div a^5 = a^{4-5} = a^{-1}$$

Raising indices to a power

To raise indices to a power you multiply the indices.

Note: As with numbers, any letter to the power of 0 is 1 so that $a^0 = 1$, $x^0 = 1$, and so on.

Like this
$$(a^4)^3 = a^{4 \times 3} = a^{12}$$

Practice Exercise

1 The area of the whole rectangle is $(x + 8)(x + 5)$.

Find the areas of the smaller rectangles that make up the whole rectangle and show that $(x + 8)(x + 5) = x^2 + 13x + 40$

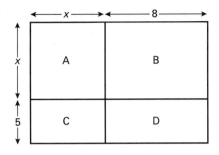

....

....

2 Why isn't $(x + 12)^2$ equal to $x^2 + 144$?

....

....

3 Expand and simplify the following expressions.

(a) $(x + 7)(x + 2)$

First .... × .... = ...

Outside .... × .... = ...

Inside .... × .... = ...

Last .... × .... = ...

Adding these and collecting like terms ....

(b) $(x - 3)(x + 8)$

....

....

(c) $(x - 5)(x - 11)$

....

....

4 Complete the following:

(a) $x^2 + 5x + 4$ $= (x + ...)(x + ...)$

(b) $x^2 + 6x - 7$ $= (x + ...)(x - ...)$

(c) $x^2 - x - 6$ $= (x ......)(x ......)$

(d) $x^2 - 11x + 24$ $= (.........)(.........)$

Algebra

Topic 5
The language of algebra

Note: You can put the plus bracket or the minus bracket first

More factorising quadratics

The difference of two squares

You must be able to recognise the difference of two squares and factorise them.

Since $(x + y)(x - y) = x^2 - xy + xy - y^2$
$$= x^2 - y^2$$

Then $\qquad x^2 - y^2 = (x + y)(x - y)$ (writing the equation the other way round)

Like this

(a) Factorise $x^2 - 16$
$x^2 - 16 = (x + 4)(x - 4)$ $\qquad$ difference of two squares where $16 = 4^2$

(b) Factorise $3x^2 - 75$
$3x^2 - 75 = 3(x^2 - 25)$ $\qquad$ as 5 is a common factor.
$\qquad\qquad = 3(x + 5)(x - 5)$ $\qquad$ difference of two squares where $25 = 5^2$

Quadratics of the form $ax^2 + bx + c$ where $a \neq 1$

To factorise quadratics of the form $ax^2 + bx + c$ you should use trial and error (with sensible numbers) to find the solution.

Like this

Factorise $11x^2 - 67x + 6$.

Since 11 only has factors 1 and 11 you can write the first terms in each bracket as
$(11x \quad)(x \quad)$

The last term is $+6$ so the two factors of $+6$ must both have plus signs or both have minus signs.

Note: You have a minus x term so you must have two minus signs.

The pairs of factors of $+6$ to try are -3 and -2, or -1 and -6.

Try $(11x - 3)(x - 2) = 11x^2 - 25x + 6$ $\qquad$ Wrong!
Try $(11x - 2)(x - 3) = 11x^2 - 35x + 6$ $\qquad$ Wrong again!
Try $(11x - 1)(x - 6) = 11x^2 - 67x + 6$ $\qquad$ Hurrah, correct!

More algebraic indices

To simplify an expression involving indices and numbers you must first work out the number part and then the letter part.

Like this

(a) Simplify $(3x^2)^3$
$(3x^2)^3 = 3^3 \times x^{2 \times 3} = 27x^6$

(b) Simplify $8x^5 \div 4x^2$
$8x^5 \div 4x^2 = (8 \div 4)x^{5-2} = 2x^3$

Negative indices

A negative index tells you to 'turn the term upside down', so a negative index gives the reciprocal.

Like this

$a^{-1} = \dfrac{1}{a}$ $\qquad a^{-3} = \dfrac{1}{a^3}$ $\qquad a^{-8} = \dfrac{1}{a^8}$ $\qquad$ and so on

Fractional indices

Fractional indices give roots.

Like this

$a^{\frac{1}{3}} \times a^{\frac{1}{3}} \times a^{\frac{1}{3}} = a^{\frac{1}{3} + \frac{1}{3} + \frac{1}{3}} = a^1 = a$

So the cube root of $a (\sqrt[3]{a})$ can be written $a^{\frac{1}{3}}$

Similarly you can write the nth root of $a (\sqrt[n]{a})$ as $a^{\frac{1}{n}}$

Practice Exercise

1 Complete the following:

(a) $4x^2 - 25 =$ $(\ldots\ldots)^2 - (\ldots\ldots)^2 = (\ldots\ldots + \ldots\ldots)(\ldots\ldots - \ldots\ldots)$

(b) $25a^2 - 16b^2 =$ $(\ldots\ldots)^2 - (\ldots\ldots)^2 = (\ldots\ldots + \ldots\ldots)(\ldots\ldots - \ldots\ldots)$

2 For each of the following choose the correct solution.

(a) $6x^2 - 7x - 5$ A $(3x + 5)(2x - 1)$
                       B $(6x - 5)(x + 1)$
                       C $(3x - 5)(2x + 1)$

2 (a) Answer ....

(b) $4x^2 - 11x - 3$ A $(2x + 1)(2x - 3)$
                       B $(4x + 1)(x - 3)$
                       C $(4x - 3)(4x + 1)$

2 (b) Answer ....

3 Factorise the following expressions:

(a) $2x^2 - 15x + 22$ $= (2x - \ldots\ldots)(x - \ldots\ldots)$

(b) $8x^2 + 10x - 3$ $= (4x\ldots\ldots)(2x\ldots\ldots)$

(c) $6x^2 + 11x - 10$ $= (\ldots\ldots)(\ldots\ldots)$

4 Here are some expressions.

$10p^3q^3$ $16(pq)^3$ $10pq^3$ $16p^3q^3$
$16p^2q^2$ $16pq^2p^2q$ $16p^2qpq^2$ $10q^3p^3$

All the expressions are meant to be simplified versions of $8pq^2 \times 2p^2q$ but some are incorrect and some are not fully simplified. Put each expression in the correct circle.

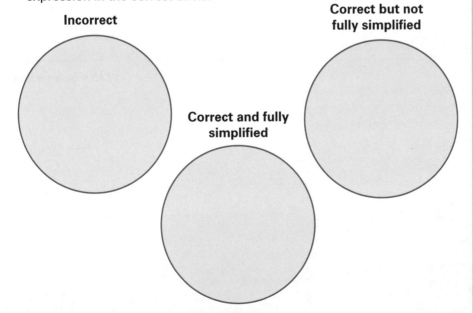

Incorrect

Correct but not fully simplified

Correct and fully simplified

Algebra

Topic 5
The language of algebra

Examination Questions

1. (a) Simplify the expressions $2x + 5y - 3x + 8y$

....

....

(b) Multiply out the expression $2(x + 5)$

....

....

(NEAB – specimen paper)

2. (a) Write down an expression for the perimeter of this rectangle

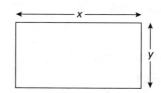

....

(b) Write down an expression for the area of this shape.

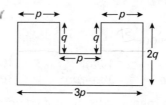

....

....

....

(NEAB – specimen paper)

3.

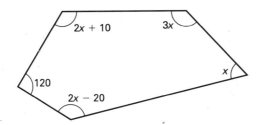

Write down and simplify an expression for the sum of the angles of this pentagon.

....

(NEAB, Summer 1998 – Paper 2H)

4. (a) Expand and simplify $(2x - 4)(x + 6)$

....

(b) Factorise

(i) $2x^2 - 4xy$

....

(ii) $x^2 + 10x - 24$

....

(NEAB, Summer 1998 – Paper 2H)

5. (a) Expand $x(3x^2 - 5)$

....

....

(b) Expand and simplify $(2x + 1)(3x - 2)$

....

(NEAB, Summer 1998 – Paper 2H)

Algebra

Topic 5

The language of algebra

Examination Questions

6. A square has sides of length $2y$ metres. A rectangle has sides of length $3y$ metres and breadth 3 metres.

(a) (i) The perimeter of the square is $2y + 2y + 2y + 2y$. Simplify this expression.

....

(ii) The perimeter of the rectangle is $3y + 3 + 3y + 3$. Simplify this expression.

....

(iii) The perimeter of the square is equal to the perimeter of the rectangle. Work out the value of y.

....

(b) The areas of these two rectangles are the same.

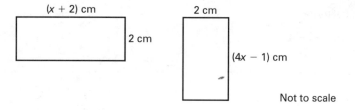

By solving the equation $2(x + 2) = 2(4x - 1)$ find the area of one of these rectangles.

....

....

(SEG – specimen paper)

7. Simplify

(a) $t^3 \times t^5$

....

(b) $p^6 \div p^2$

....

(c) $\dfrac{a^3 \times a^2}{a}$

....

(NEAB, Summer 1998 – Paper 11)

Examination Questions

8. (a) x is a number which is greater than 1. List the following four terms in order of size, smallest first.

$$x^{-2} \qquad x \qquad x^{\frac{1}{2}} \qquad \frac{1}{x}$$

....

....

(b) If $0 < x < 1$, how should your list in part a be re-arranged, if at all?

....

....

(NEAB, 1998 – Higher Paper 1H)

9. The expression $\dfrac{1}{\sqrt{a}} = a^n$ is true for all values of a. Find the value of n.

....

(NEAB, 1998 – Higher Paper 1H)

Topic 6 Making graphs

Summary

Cartesian co-ordinates in four quadrants

You can extend the axes of a graph to include both positive and negative numbers. Each co-ordinate must consist of two numbers separated by a comma in a pair of brackets.

Like this

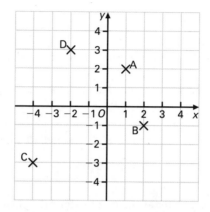

A (1, 2)
B (2, −1)
C (−4, −3)
D (−2, 3)

Note: *Remember that the first number of the co-ordinate gives the distance along the x axis from the origin and the second number gives the distance along the y axis from the origin.*

Plotting straight-line graphs

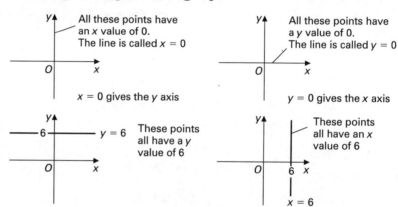

All these points have an x value of 0.
The line is called $x = 0$
$x = 0$ gives the y axis

All these points have a y value of 0.
The line is called $y = 0$
$y = 0$ gives the x axis

$y = 6$ These points all have a y value of 6

These points all have an x value of 6
$x = 6$

To plot more difficult lines you need to make a **table of values**.

You must choose your x values and work out the corresponding y values.

Like this

Draw the line $y = 3x - 1$

You start by choosing some x values to plot – in this case −3, 0 and 3 are suitable x values – and then produce a table to show the corresponding y values. The table of values would look like this:

x	−3	0	3
$y = 3x - 1$	−10	−1	8
(x, y)	(−3, −10)	(0, −1)	(3, 8)

You can now draw a set of axes (using a suitable scale) and plot the points.

Join the points up with a straight line.

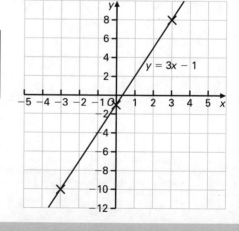

$y = 3x - 1$

Note: *Although you need only two points to define a straight line, it is always best to plot three points in case you've made a mistake.*

Practice Exercise

1 (a) Write down the co-ordinates of the points in each diagram.

(i)

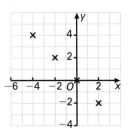

(ii)

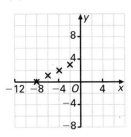

(iii)

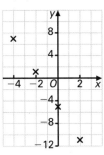

(b) Find another point on each of the lines.

2 Plot the following points and join them in order: (1, 4), (2, 4), (2, −3), (1, −3), (−2, 2), (−2, −3), (−3, −3), (−3, 4), (−2, 4), (1, −1), (1, 4).

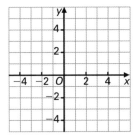

3 On the same axes draw

(a) $y = 2x$
$y = 3x$
$y = 5x$

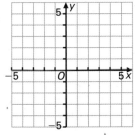

(b) $y = -2x$
$y = -3x$
$y = -5x$

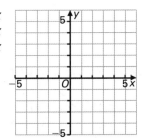

(c) $y = x + 1$
$y = x + 3$
$y = x - 2$

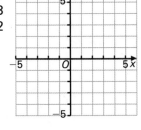

(d) $y = 2x + 3$
$y = 2x + 4$
$y = 2x - 1$

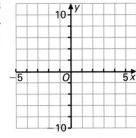

(e) What do you notice in each case?

....

....

....

....

1 (a) (i) Answer

(......, ...) (......, ...)

(......, ...) (......, ...)

1 (a) (ii) Answer

(......, ...) (......, ...)

(......, ...) (......, ...)

1 (a) (iii) Answer

(......, ...) (......, ...)

(......, ...) (......, ...)

1 (b) (i) Answer (......, ...)

1 (b) (ii) Answer (......, ...)

1 (b) (iii) Answer (......, ...)

Algebra

Topic 6 Making graphs

Note: In this case the x values of the points to be plotted are given. If they are not given you need to make a sensible choice of x values to use.

Note: Check that your points do form a smooth line. If a point seems misplaced then check again.

Plotting curves

To draw curves you need to make a **table of values**.
You must choose your x values and work out the corresponding y values.

Like this

Draw the curve $y = \dfrac{8}{x}$ between -8 and $+8$ on the x axis.

x	-8	-6	-4	-2	0	2	4	6	8
$y = \dfrac{8}{x}$	-1	-1.3	-2	-4	error	4	2	1.3	1
(x, y)	$(-8, -1)$	$(-6, -1.3)$	$(-4, -2)$	$(-2, -4)$		$(2, 4)$	$(4, 2)$	$(6, 1.3)$	$(8, 1)$

Since it is not easy to see what is going on around $x = 0$, it may be helpful to choose some extra x values.

x	-1	$-\frac{1}{2}$	$\frac{1}{2}$	1
$y = \dfrac{8}{x}$	-8	-16	16	8
(x, y)	$(-1, -8)$	$(-\frac{1}{2}, -16)$	$(\frac{1}{2}, 16)$	$(1, 8)$

You can now draw a set of axes (using a suitable scale) and plot the points. Join the points up with a smooth curve.

The graph $y = \dfrac{8}{x}$ has two separate parts, so in this case you need to join your points with two smooth curves.

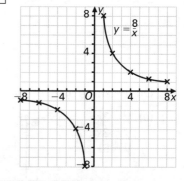

Sketching curves

If you are asked to sketch a graph then you do not need to draw the graph accurately. You should just 'sketch' the shape of the curve and show whether or not it passes through the origin. You may also need to show values where your graph crosses the axes.

Quadratic graphs

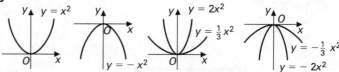

Cubic graphs

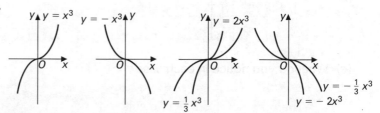

Reciprocal graphs

(where k is a constant)

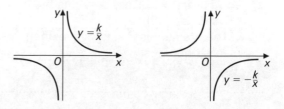

Note: Remember that reciprocal graphs come in two parts.

Practice Exercise

1 On the same axes draw:

(a) $y = x^2$
$y = x^2 + 3$
$y = x^2 - 1$

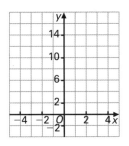

(b) $y = x^3$
$y = x^3 + 4$
$y = x^3 - 2$

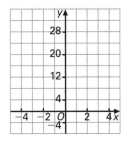

(c) $y = \dfrac{1}{x}$
$y = \dfrac{3}{x}$
$y = \dfrac{4}{x}$

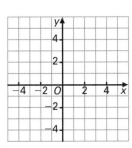

(d) $y = -\dfrac{1}{x}$
$y = -\dfrac{3}{x}$
$y = -\dfrac{4}{x}$

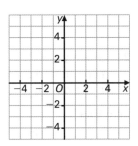

(e) What do you notice?

....

....

....

....

2 Match each description with the correct function.

(a)
> The graph of this function does not cut either of the axes and its gradient is always negative.

A $y = (x - 2)(x - 3)$

2 (a) Answer ....

(b)
> The graph of this function has a gradient which is never negative. The graph goes through the origin.

B $y = \dfrac{2}{x}$

2 (b) Answer ....

(c)
> The graph of this function cuts the x-axis in two places and cuts the y-axis at $(0, 6)$.
> The gradient is first negative, then zero, then positive.

C $y = x^3$

2 (c) Answer ....

Topic 6
Making
graphs

Summary

Transformations using graphs

You must be able to 'do' the following six transformations for any given graph $y = f(x)$.

1 Given $y = f(x)$, sketch $y = f(x) + a$.
You must move the given graph a units in the direction of the positive y axis.

Like this
Given $y = f(x)$, sketch $y = f(x) + 1$ and $y = f(x) - 2$.

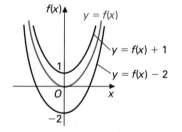

2 Given $y = f(x)$, sketch $y = f(x - a)$.
You must move the given graph a units in the direction of the positive x axis.

Like this
Given $y = f(x)$, sketch $y = f(x - 2)$
and $y = f(x + 1)$.

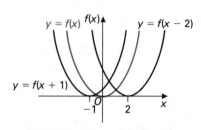

3 Given $y = f(x)$, sketch $y = -f(x)$
You must reflect the given graph in the x axis.

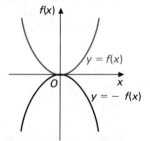

4 Given $y = f(x)$, sketch $y = f(-x)$
You must reflect the given graph in the y axis.

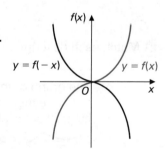

5 Given $y = f(x)$, sketch $y = af(x)$
You must stretch the given graph in the direction of the y axis by multiplying y values by a.

Like this
Given $y = f(x)$, sketch $2f(x)$ and $y = \frac{1}{2}f(x)$.

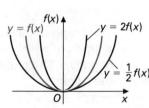

6 Given $y = f(x)$, sketch $y = f(ax)$
You must 'squash' the given graph in the direction of the x axis by multiplying x values by a.

Like this
Given $y = f(x)$, sketch $y = f(3x)$ and $y = f(\frac{1}{2}x)$.

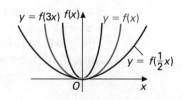

Practice Exercise

1 Here is a sketch of a function $f(x)$.

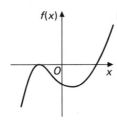

Draw sketches of:

(a) $2f(x)$

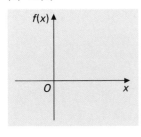

(b) $f(x + 2)$

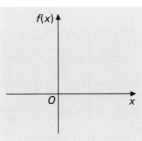

(c) $f(2x)$

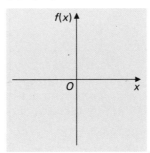

2 (a) On these axes, draw sketches of $y = \sin x$, $y = \sin 2x$ and $y = 2 \sin x$. Label each of your curves clearly.

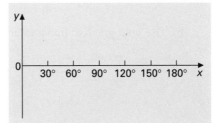

(b) On these axes, draw sketches of $y = \sin x$, $y = \sin (-x)$ and $y = -2 \sin x$. Label each of your curves clearly.

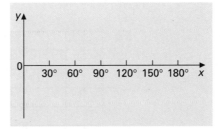

(c) On these axes, draw sketches of $y = \sin x$, $y = \sin (x + 90°)$ and $y = \sin (x - 180°)$. Label each of your curves clearly.

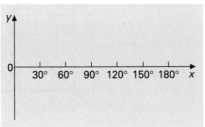

Topic 6
Making graphs

1. (a) Draw the graph of $y = 2x^2$ for values of x from 0 to 3.

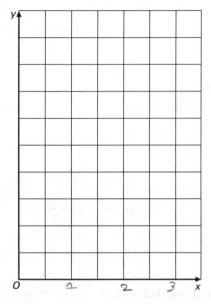

(b) Use your graph to find a value of x when $y = 12$.

....

(SEG, Summer 1997 – Intermediate Paper 3, part question)

2. The following graph shows the line $y = 2x + 8$

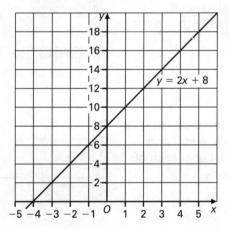

On the same graph draw the curve $y = x^2$

Write down the points of intersection of the straight line $y = 2x + 8$ and the curve $y = x^2$

Co-ordinates are (........., ...) and (........., ...)

Algebra

Topic 6
Making
graphs

Intermediate and Higher Tiers

Higher Tier Only

Examination Questions

3. The cross-section of a swimming pool is shown. It is filled, from empty, at a uniform rate. Sketch a graph of the water height against time, t, as the pool fills.

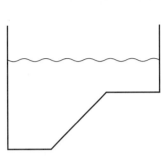

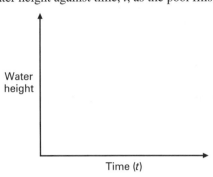

(SEG, Summer 1997 – Higher Paper 6)

4. The function $y = f(x)$ is illustrated.

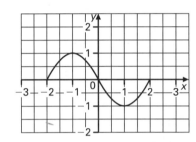

(a) On the axes below sketch

   (i) $y = 2f(x)$ (ii) $y = f(x - 1)$

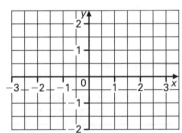 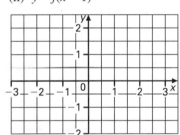

(b) Which one of these sketches is of the form $y = f(x) + a$ where a is a constant? What is the value of a?

A 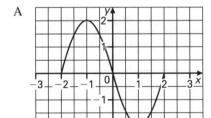   B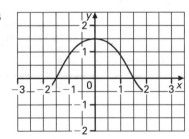

C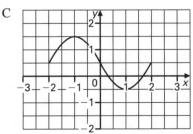

(SEG, Summer 1997 – Higher Paper 6)

Algebra

Topic 7
Using graphs

Note: *The gradient, i.e. 'steepness', of the travel graph shows the speed. The steeper the line, the greater the speed.*

Real-life graphs

You need to be able to plot and draw graphs of everyday situations such as travel graphs.

Travel graphs

Travel graphs are very popular on examination papers. They show time on the horizontal axis against distance on the vertical axis.

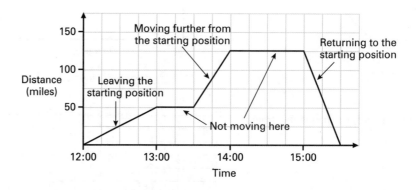

Inequalities and number lines

You must be able to use a number line to show an inequality.

Like this

Show the following inequalities on a number line:

(a) $x > 5$

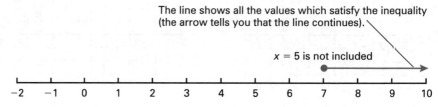

The line shows all the values which satisfy the inequality (the arrow tells you that the line continues).

$x = 5$ is not included

Note: *A closed circle means the number at the end of the range is included. An open circle means the number is not included.*

(b) $-3 < x \leq 0$

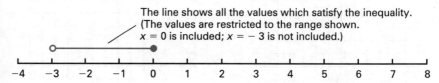

The line shows all the values which satisfy the inequality. (The values are restricted to the range shown. $x = 0$ is included; $x = -3$ is not included.)

Practice Exercise

1 Here is a distance–time graph. Which description fits the graph?

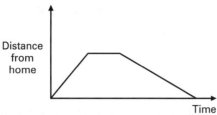

Distance from home

Time

A Sally sets off from home walks up a hill across the top and down the other side.

B Sally sets off from home, increases her speed, goes at a steady speed for a while then slows down and stops.

C Sally travels at a steady speed, stops for a rest then returns home at a slower speed than before.

D Sally sets off from home, goes at a steady speed for a while, stops for a rest and then sets off in the same direction.

1 Answer ....

2 Complete the graph to show the following information:
A cyclist leaves Croyston at 12.00 noon and cycles to Darley 40 km away. The cyclist arrived at Darley at 2.00 pm. A motorist leaves Croyston at 12.30 pm and travels to Darley at a steady speed of 60 km/h.

From your graph:

(a) When does the motorist pass the cyclist?

(b) What time does the motorist arrive in Darley?

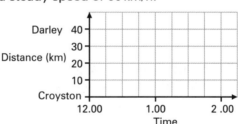

2 (a) Answer ....

2 (b) Answer ....

3 Show the following inequalities on this number line.

(a) $a \geq 5$ (b) $b \leq -3$ (c) $c > -2$ (d) $-3 \leq d < 8$

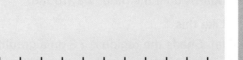

4 Write down the inequalities shown on the number lines.

(a)

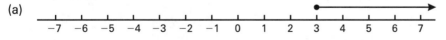

4 (a) Answer ....

(b)

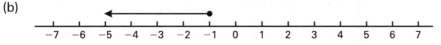

4 (b) Answer ....

(c)

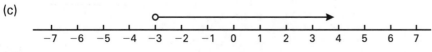

4 (c) Answer ....

(d)

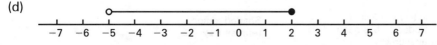

4 (d) Answer ....

Algebra

Topic 7
Using graphs

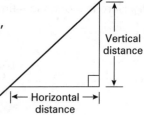

Summary

Gradient of a line

The gradient of a line is a measure of its 'steepness.'

$$\text{Gradient} = \frac{\text{vertical distance}}{\text{horizontal distance}}$$

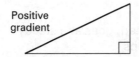

Gradients are positive if the slope is 'uphill' or negative if the slope is 'downhill.'

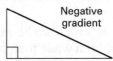

Positive gradient

Negative gradient

The general equation of a straight line ($y = mx + c$)

The equation of any straight line can be written in the form $y = mx + c$ where m is the gradient of the line and c is where the line cuts the y axis (i.e. c is the intercept on the y axis).

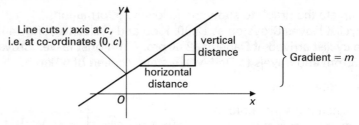

Line cuts y axis at c, i.e. at co-ordinates $(0, c)$

vertical distance

horizontal distance

Gradient = m

To find the equation of a given straight line you have to work out the gradient and find the value of y where the line cuts the y axis. Simple!

You then have $y = \text{gradient} \times x + \text{value where line cuts the } y \text{ axis}$.

Inequalities and graphs

To show inequalities on a graph you must first plot the boundary line. You usually shade the region you don't want, but remember to **read the question carefully** to make sure. Just to keep you on your toes, some exam boards do it the other way round!

Like this

(a) Shade the region $x > 3$ on a graph.

(b) Shade the region $y \leqslant 2$ on a graph.

(c) Shade the region satisfied by $x < 2$ and $y \geqslant -1$ on a graph.

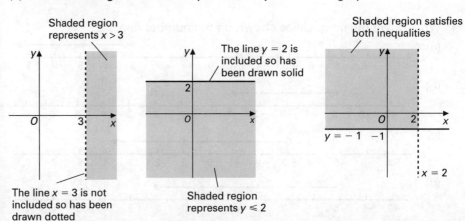

Shaded region represents $x > 3$

The line $x = 3$ is not included so has been drawn dotted

The line $y = 2$ is included so has been drawn solid

Shaded region represents $y \leqslant 2$

Shaded region satisfies both inequalities

Note: To find the gradient of a straight line you should choose two points on your line and create a right-angled triangle with sides parallel to the axes. It is best if you can choose your two points as far apart as possible so that the triangle you draw is quite large.

Note: Always check whether the gradient is positive or negative.

Note: If the line goes through the origin then $c = 0$ and $y = \text{gradient} \times x$.

Note: Read the question carefully. Does the question ask you to shade the region required or the region not required?

Practice Exercise

1. Arrange these lines in order of their gradients, smallest gradient first.

   $y = 2x + 3$ .... Smallest gradient

   $y = \dfrac{x}{2} + 10$ ....

   $3y = x - 1$ ....

   $5y = 8x$ .... Largest gradient

 Which graph corresponds to each of these equations.

   (a) $y = 2.5$

   (b) $x + y = 3$

   (c) $y = 2x$

   (d) $y = \frac{1}{2}x + 1$

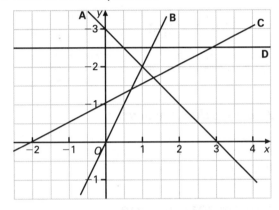

   2 (a) Answer ....

   2 (b) Answer ....

   2 (c) Answer ....

   2 (d) Answer ....

3. Show clearly on the diagram the region where all these inequalities are satisfied:

   $y \geqslant 0 \qquad y \leqslant 2x \qquad x + y \leqslant 4$

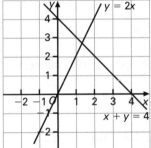

4. For each of the following equations identify the gradient (m) and the intercept on the y axis (c).

   (a) $y = 3x + 2$ $m =$ .... $c =$ ....

   (b) $y = -2x + 7$ $m =$ .... $c =$ ....

   (c) $y = 2x - \frac{1}{2}$ $m =$ .... $c =$ ....

   (d) $2y = x + 2$ $m =$ .... $c =$ ....

   (e) $2x + y = 3$ $m =$ .... $c =$ ....

Topic 7
Using graphs

Note: *The gradient of the tangent to the curve will be different depending on the point used.*

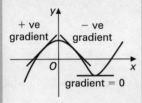

Note: *The area of a trapezium is* $\frac{h}{2}(a+b)$

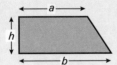

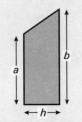

Summary

Gradients and curves

It is not possible to find the gradient of a curve.

However the gradient at any given point on a curve can be found by drawing a **tangent** at the point and finding its gradient.

The units of the gradient (i.e. vertical units/horizontal units) will give you an idea of what the gradient represents.

tangent to curve at point A

curve

Like this

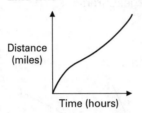

gradient = miles/hour
gradient measures speed

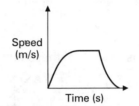

gradient = metres per second/ second
gradient measures acceleration

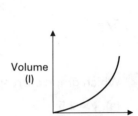

gradient = litres/minute
gradient measures flow rate

Area under a curve

You can find the approximate area under a curve by adding up individual squares or else by approximating the area of a series of rectangles or trapezia (plural for trapezium).

The trapezium rule

The trapezium rule allows you to find an approximation for the area under a curve.

Like this

Find the area under the curve $y = x^2$ between $x = 2$ and $x = 6$.

Draw the graph and construct a series of trapezia.

Area under graph

$$= T_1 + T_2 + T_3 + T_4$$
$$= \tfrac{1}{2}(4 + 9) + \tfrac{1}{2}(9 + 16) + \tfrac{1}{2}(16 + 25)$$
$$+ \tfrac{1}{2}(25 + 36)$$
$$= 6.5 + 12.5 + 20.5 + 30.5$$
$$= 70 \text{ square units}$$

The units of the area (vertical units $\times$ horizontal units) will give you an idea of what the area represents.

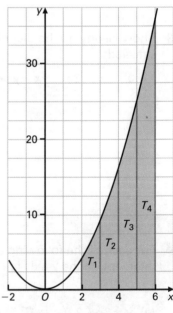

Like this

Area = metres per second $\times$ seconds
    = metres
Area measures distance travelled

Shaded area represents distance travelled in metres between 10 and 40 seconds

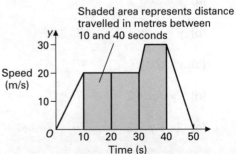

Practice Exercise

1 Use the speed–time graph to decide whether each statement is true or false.

(a) For the shaded area the average speed is $10\,\text{ms}^{-1}$

(b) For the shaded area the average acceleration is $1\,\text{ms}^{-2}$

(c) The acceleration at 5 seconds is represented by the gradient of AB

(d) The total distance travelled in 20 s is 400 m

(e) The distance travelled between 5 seconds and 15 seconds is represented by the shaded area

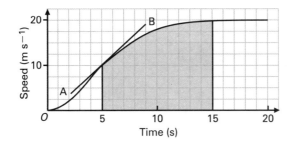

1 (a) Answer ....

1 (b) Answer ....

1 (c) Answer ....

1 (d) Answer ....

1 (e) Answer ....

2 A researcher collects some data of two variables, x and y, in an experiment. She suspects that the data should fit the equation $y = px^2 + q$.

(a) Which of these should produce a straight line graph?

 A Plotting y^2 against x^2

 B Plotting y against x

 C Plotting y against x^2

 D Plotting y^2 against x

2 (a) Answer ....

(b) Explain how to find the values of p and q when the correct graph has been plotted.

....

....

3 Draw the graph of $y = x^2 + x - 6$ on the axes below.

Use your graph to find the solutions of the equation $x^2 + x - 6 = 0$

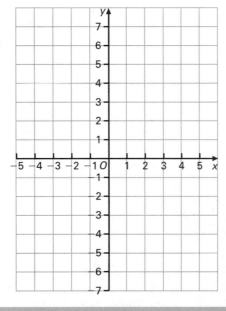

3 Answer

$x = $ ...., $x = $ ....

Topic 7
Using graphs

Examination Questions

1. Jane takes 15 minutes to walk half a mile from home to the bus stop. She waits at the bus stop for 5 minutes then catches the bus. The bus takes 15 minutes to travel the two miles to school.

Draw a distance–time graph to show Jane's journey to school.

2. (a) On the diagram draw and label the following lines.

$y = 2x$ and $x + y = 5$

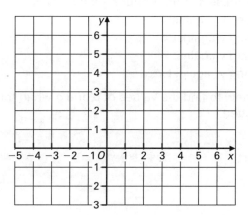

(b) Explain how to use your graph to solve the equation $2x = 5 - x$

....

....

(c) Show clearly the single region that is satisfied by **all** of these inequalities

$$x + y \leq 5 \qquad y \geq 2x \qquad x \geq 0$$

Label the region R.

(SEG, Summer 1998 – Intermediate Paper 14)

3. The distance from Upton to Dorchester is 20 miles.

   The diagram shows the distance–time graph of a cyclist travelling from Upton to Dorchester.

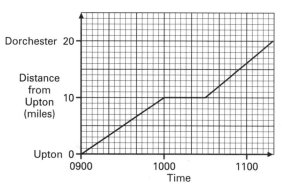

   At 0940 a motorist leaves Dorchester to travel to Upton along the same road as the cyclist. The motorist travels at an average speed of 40 mph.

   (a)   On the same diagram draw the distance–time graph of the motorist.

   (b)   At what time did the motorist pass the cyclist?

   ....

   (SEG, Summer 1997 – Intermediate Paper 3)

4. The diagram shows the graph of $y = x^3$. By drawing the graph $y = x^2 + 1$ for $0 \leqslant x \leqslant 2$, estimate the solution of the equation $x^3 = x^2 + 1$.

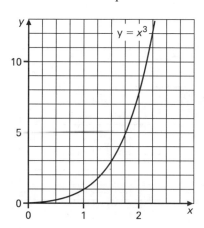

   *(SEG, Summer 1997 – Higher Paper 6)*Algebra

Examination Questions

5. (a) Below are three graphs.
    Match each graph with one of the following equations.

    Equation A: $y = 3x - p$
    Equation B: $y = x^2 + p$
    Equation C: $3x + 4y = p$
    Equation D: $y = px^3$

    In each case p is a positive number

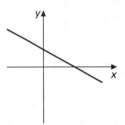 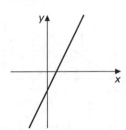 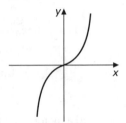

    (b) Sketch a graph of the equation you have not yet chosen.

(NEAB, Summer 1998 – Higher Paper 2)

6. (a) Draw the graph of $y = x^2 - 3x$ for values of x from -1 to 4.

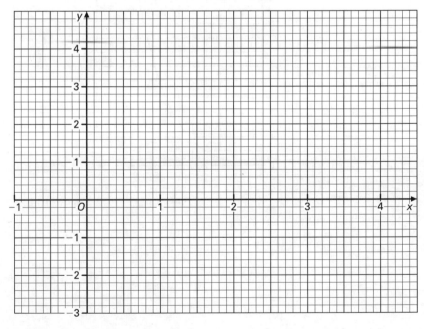

    (b) By drawing a suitable straight line on the same diagram, estimate, correct to
        one decimal place, the solutions to the equation $x^2 - 2x - 1 = 0$.

    (c) By drawing another straight line on the same diagram, solve the inequality
        $x^2 - 3x \leqslant 1$

(SEG – Specimen Higher Paper)

Examination Questions

7. A ball is rolled down a slide and along a table.

The table has a smooth surface and a rough surface.

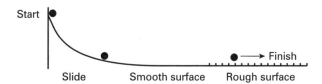

Start • ⌐

Slide   Smooth surface   Rough surface   → Finish

The ball takes 8 seconds from start to finish.

The velocity *v* metres per second at time *t* seconds at each stage is shown on the graph.

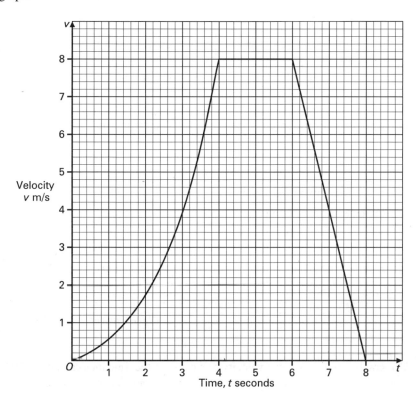

(a) Estimate the acceleration of the ball when $t = 1.5$

....

State the units of acceleration.

....

(b) Estimate the total distance travelled by the ball.

....

(NEAB, Summer 1998 – Higher Paper 2H)

Topic 7
Using graphs

Examination Questions

8. The graph illustrates the journey of a London Underground train between two stations. The journey takes 100 seconds.

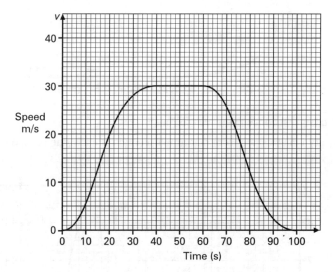

(a) Describe how the speed of the train varies on the journey.

....

....

(b) Estimate the maximum acceleration of the train.

....

(c) Estimate the distance in kilometres between the stations.

....

(SEG, Summer 1997 – Higher Paper 6)

9. The graph below shows the velocity of a car over the time interval $0 < t < 20$, where t is time in seconds and v is the velocity in metres per second.

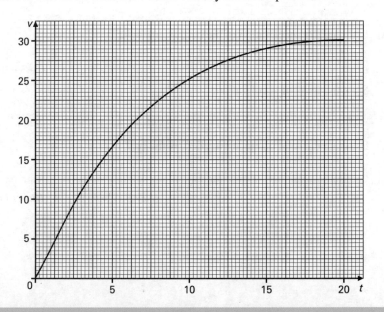

(a) Use the graph to estimate the acceleration of the car at $t = 7.5$

....

(b) (i) Estimate the area under the graph for the interval $0 \leqslant t \leqslant 10$.

....

(ii) What does this area represent?

....

(SEG – Specimen Higher Paper)

10. (a) The diagram shows the graph of $y = \cos x$ for $0° \leqslant x \leqslant 360°$.

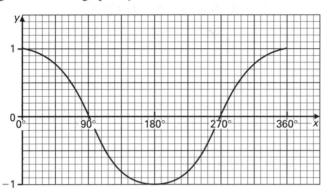

(i) On the diagram show the location of the two solutions of the equation $\cos x = -0.5$

(ii) The angle x is between $0°$ and $360°$. Work out accurately the two solutions of the equation $\cos x = -0.5$

....

....

(b) On a particular day the height, h metres, of the tide at Weymouth, relative to a certain point, can be modelled by the equation $h = 5 \sin(30t)°$, where t is the time after midnight.

(i) On the axes below sketch the graph of h against t for $0 \leqslant t \leqslant 12$.

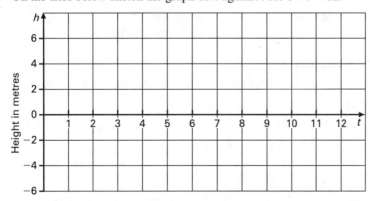

(ii) Estimate the height of the tide, relative to the same point, at 2 pm that day.

....

(SEG – Specimen Higher Paper 15)

Algebra

Topic 8
Using algebra

Note: *Once you have made your equation you should be able to solve it! This means finding the value of x (the number of tickets sold) which works in the equation.*

Summary

Making equations

Sometimes you can solve a problem by writing an equation.

Like this

(a) It costs £50 to hire a hall for a disco (you provide the music!). If you sell x tickets at £1.50 each, write an expression for your profit, P, in £s.

You make £1.50 $\times x$ from selling the tickets, but you have to subtract the cost of hiring the hall from your profit. So
$P = 1.5x - 50$

(b) If your profit is £250, write an equation for x.
Your equation is $1.5x - 50 = 250$

Rules for solving linear equations

1 What you do to one side of an equation you must do to the other side. Think of your equation as a balance.

Like this

Solve $1.5x - 50 = 250$
To get the x term by itself add 50 to each side $1.5x = 300$
Now to get x divide each side by 1.5 $x = 200$

2 You must collect all the x terms on one side of the equation and the number terms on the other side.

Like this

Solve $9x + 8 = 7x - 3$

Subtract $7x$ from both sides $9x - 7x + 8 = 7x - 7x - 3$
$2x + 8 = -3$

Subtract 8 from both sides $2x + 8 - 8 = -3 - 8$
$2x = -11$

Divide both sides by 2 $x = -\dfrac{11}{2} = -5.5$

3 If you have any brackets you must get rid of them!

Like this

Solve $3(x + 2) = 4(x - 1)$
Work out the brackets $3x + 6 = 4x - 4$
Subtract $3x$ from both sides $3x - 3x + 6 = 4x - 3x - 4$
$6 = x - 4$

Add 4 to both sides $6 + 4 = x - 4 + 4$
$10 = x$ or $x = 10$

Note: *It is easier to work on the side which keeps the x term positive.*

Substitution

Remember that substitution is where you replace a letter by a given number.

Like this

If $a = 2$, $b = -3$ and $c = \frac{1}{2}$ find the values of $3a + 4c$, $3a - 5b$, abc, $\dfrac{b}{c}$, and b^a.

$3a + 4c = 3 \times 2 + 4 \times \frac{1}{2} = 6 + 2 = 8$

$3a - 5b = 3 \times 2 - 5 \times -3 = 6 + 15 = 21$ remember that $- \times - = +$

$abc = 2 \times -3 \times \frac{1}{2} = -3$

$\dfrac{b}{c} = \dfrac{-3}{\frac{1}{2}} = -6$

$ba = (-3)^2 = -3 \times -3 = 9$

Practice Exercise

1 Find the weight of one of the unknown containers in each of parts a–f. Where there is more than one unknown container, you may assume they are of equal weight.

(a)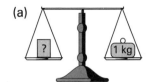

(b)

(c)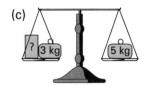

(d)

(e)

(f)

1 (a) Answer ....kg

1 (b) Answer ....kg

1 (c) Answer ....kg

1 (d) Answer ....kg

1 (e) Answer ....kg

1 (f) Answer ....kg

2 Which two of these equations have got the same solution?

A $3x - 6 = 9$

B $2x = 2.5$

C $\dfrac{x}{2} = 2.5$

D $3(x - 6) = 9$

2 Answer .... and ....

3 A quadrilateral has three angles of $x°$ and one angle of 75°. Make an equation to show this information and solve it to find the value of x.

....

....

4 If $a = 3$, $b = 2$, $c = \frac{1}{2}$, $d = -\frac{1}{3}$ then connect the expression to its answer. The first one has been done for you.

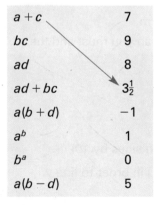

$a + c$	7
bc	9
ad	8
$ad + bc$	$3\frac{1}{2}$
$a(b + d)$	-1
a^b	1
b^a	0
$a(b - d)$	5

Topic 8
Using algebra

Summary

Solving quadratic equations

Quadratic equations can be solved using the fact that if $A \times B = 0$, then either $A = 0$ or $B = 0$ (or both $A = 0$ and $B = 0$).

Like this

Solve $(x - 5)(x + 2) = 0$

Since $(x - 5)(x + 2)$ is the same as $(x - 5) \times (x + 2)$ then either $(x - 5) = 0$ or $(x + 2) = 0$

If $(x - 5) = 0$ then $x = 5$ and if $(x + 2) = 0$ then $x = -2$

So the solutions are $x = 5$ or $x = -2$

Quadratics of the form $ax^2 + bx + c = 0$ should be factorised and then solved in a similar manner.

Like this

Solve $x^2 - 3x - 10 = 0$

Factorising the left-hand side you get $(x - 5)(x + 2)$

So $(x - 5)(x + 2) = 0$ and you proceed as above.

Simultaneous linear equations

Simultaneous equations are two equations which have two unknown terms. You need to find the two answers which 'work' for both equations.

Like this

Solve the simultaneous equations $4x + y = 7$ and $2x - 2y = 11$.

Step 1 Label the equations. $4x + y = 7$ [1]
$2x - 2y = 11$ [2]   No sweat yet!

Step 2 Choose to make the number in front of either the x or y term the same in both equations. In this case make the y terms the same by multiplying both sides of equation [1] by 2.

This gives $8x + 2y = 14$ [1] $\times$ 2
and you still have $2x - 2y = 11$ [2]

Note: You could choose to make the x terms the same by multiplying equation [2] by 2.

Step 3 You must now get rid of your chosen term.

The chosen y terms have different signs so you must add the equations to get rid of these terms.

$8x + 2y = 14$
add $2x - 2y = 11$
$10x = 25$

Note: If the chosen terms have the same signs, subtract the two equations. If the chosen terms have different signs, add the two equations.

Step 4 Now find x. $10x = 25$
$x = 2.5$ (dividing both sides by 10)

Step 5 Substitute the value of x into equation [1] in order to find y.
$4x + y = 7$ [1]
$4 \times 2.5 + y = 7$
$y = -3$

Note: It is sensible to check your answers by substituting the values of x and y into equation [2];
$2x - 2y$
$= 2 \times 2.5 - 2 \times -3$
$= 5 + 6 = 11$

You can also solve simultaneous equations using graphs. Plot graphs for the two equations you need to solve. The point of intersection of the two graphs (x, y) gives the solutions of the two simultaneous equations. If the graphs do not intersect, then the simultaneous equations have no solution.

Practice Exercise

1 Solve the following equations

(a) $(x-3)(x+7) = 0$

Either (..................) = 0 or (..................) = 0

So $x =$ ....   or $x =$ ....

(b) $(x+7)(2x-5) = 0$

Either (..................) = 0 or (..................) = 0

So $x =$ ....   or $x =$ ....

(c) $x^2 + 2x - 15 = 0$

$(x +$ ....$)$ $(x -$ ....$) = 0$

Either $(x +$ ....$) = 0$ or $(x -$ ....$) = 0$

So $x =$ ....   or $x =$ ....

(d) $x^2 - 3x - 28 = 0$

(..................) (..................) = 0

Either (..................) = 0 or (..................) = 0

So $x =$ ....   or $x =$ ....

2 Match the equations and the solutions, then solve the equation left over.

$x^2 + 7x + 12 = 0$

$\qquad$ $x = 4, x = 3$

$x^2 + x - 12 = 0$

$\qquad$ $x = -4, x = 3$

$x^2 - x - 12 = 0$

$\qquad$ $x = 4, x = -3$

$x^2 - 7x - 12 = 0$

2 Answer x = ...

x = ...

3 Solve the simultaneous equations:

(a) $2x + y = 11$
     $5x - 2y = 5$

(b) $2x + y = 1$
     $x - 2y = 8$

3 (a) Answer x = ..., y = ...

3 (b) Answer x = ..., y = ...

Topic 8
Using algebra

More difficult quadratic equations

Not all quadratic equations can be solved by factorising. Sometimes the quadratic equation doesn't factorise. You can solve quadratic equations that do not factorise using the **quadratic formula**:

$$x = \frac{-b \pm \sqrt{b^2 - 4ac}}{2a}$$

The quadratic formula can be used to solve quadratic equations of the form $ax^2 + bx + c = 0$

Like this

Solve $3x^2 + 5x - 1 = 0$

Compare $3x^2 + 5x - 1 = 0$
with $ax^2 + bx + c = 0$
So $a = 3$, $b = 5$ and $c = -1$

You now substitute $a = 3$, $b = 5$ and $c = -1$ into the quadratic formula (simple!).

$$x = \frac{-b \pm \sqrt{b^2 - 4ac}}{2a}$$

$$x = \frac{-5 \pm \sqrt{5^2 - 4 \times 3 \times -1}}{2 \times 3}$$

$$x = \frac{-5 \pm \sqrt{37}}{6}$$

The $\pm$ means that you have to work out the formula twice, once using the $+$ and once using the $-$.

$$x = \frac{-5 + \sqrt{37}}{6} \qquad\qquad x = \frac{-5 - \sqrt{37}}{6}$$

$x = 0.180\,(3\,dp)$ or $x = -1.847\,(3\,dp)$

You can also solve quadratic equations using graphical methods. Plot the quadratic equation you need to solve. The intersection of the graph with the x axis gives the solutions to the equation $ax^2 + bx + c = 0$.

Practice Exercise

1 Solve the equation $3x^2 + 5x - 2 = 0$ using the quadratic formula.

....

....

....

....

....

....

1 Answer x = ...

or x = ...

Note: *This equation could have been more easily solved by factorising.*

2 Solve the equation $5x^2 + 6x - 4 = 0$ using the quadratic formula.
Give your answers to 3 sf.

....

....

....

....

....

....

2 Answer x = ... *(3 sf)*

or x = ... *(3 sf)*

3 Write down one quadratic equation that can be solved by factorising and one that does not factorise. Solve the equation that does not factorise, using the quadratic formula.

....

....

....

....

....

....

....

Algebra

Topic 8
Using algebra

Examination Questions

1. Solve the equation $2(3x + 5) = 4x + 7$

....

....

(SEG, Summer 1997 – Intermediate Paper 4)

2. P and Q are rectangles.
The dimensions are given in centimetres.

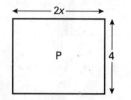

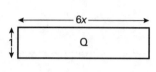

(a) (i)   Write down a simplified expression for the area of P.

....

(ii)   What is the perimeter of P in centimetres?

....

The two rectangles have the same perimeter.
The perimeter of P is $4x + 8$.
The perimeter of Q is $12x + 2$

(b)   Solve the equation $4x + 8 = 12x + 2$

....

....

(SEG, Summer 1997 – Intermediate Paper 3)

3. The height, h metres, of a stone t seconds after being thrown in the air is given by the formula

$$h = ut + \tfrac{1}{2}at^2$$

Find the height of the stone after 5 seconds when $u = 12.9$ and $a = -9.8$

....

....

4. Solve these simultaneous equations $4x + 5y = 5$
$$2x - y = 6$$

....

....

....

....

Do not use a trial and improvement method.

(NEAB, Summer 1998 – Higher Paper 2H)

5. Find, correct to 2 decimal places, the solutions of the equation $x^2 - 2x - 1 = 0$

   Working must be shown. Do not use a trial and improvement method.

   ....

   ....

   ....

   ....

   (NEAB, Summer 1998 – Higher Paper 2H)

6.

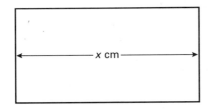

   The perimeter of this rectangle is 20 cm. The length of this rectangle is x cm. The area of the rectangle is 11 cm².

   (a) Form an equation in x and show that the equation can be simplified to the form $x^2 - 10x + 11 = 0$

   ....

   ....

   (b) Solve this equation to find the length and width of the rectangle. Give your answer to an appropriate degree of accuracy.

   ....

   ....

   ....

   ....

   (SEAG – Specimen Higher Paper)

Algebra

Topic 9
More using algebra

Summary

Sequences using the method of 'add one'

In the sequence 7, 10, 13, ... to find the next term you 'add on 3' each time.
The next two terms are 16 and 19.

The nth term is $7 + 3(n - 1) = 7 + 3n - 3 = 4 + 3n$

In general if there is an 'add on' or difference of d between each term, then

nth term = first term + $d \times (n - 1)$

Like this

Find the next two terms and the nth term in the sequence: $-2, 2, 6, ...$

To find the next term you 'add on 4' each time.

The next two terms are 10 $(6 + 4)$ and 14 $(10 + 4)$.

nth term $= $ first term $+ d \times (n - 1)$

$$\begin{aligned} n\text{th term} &= -2 + (n - 1) \times \text{difference} \\ &= -2 + (n - 1) \times 4 \\ &= -2 + 4n - 4 \\ &= -6 + 4n \quad \text{or} \quad 4n - 6 \end{aligned}$$

Solving linear inequalities

To solve linear inequalities you use the same procedure as solving linear equations except when you multiply or divide by a negative number. When you multiply or divide by a negative number you must change the direction of the inequality.

You have $\qquad 3 > 1$

Multiply by $-1 \qquad -3 < -1$

You must change the direction of the inequality to make the statement correct.

Transforming or changing the subject of formulae

This is a fancy way of saying find one letter in terms of another letter (or other letters).

You must isolate the letter term you want on one side of the formula. The rules of linear equations apply!

Like this

(a) Find t given that $v = u + at$

Subtract u from both sides to isolate the t term $\qquad v - u = at$

Divide both sides by a to get t by itself $\qquad \dfrac{v - u}{a} = t$

Turn the equation around to make t the subject $\qquad t = \dfrac{v - u}{a}$

(b) Find r, the radius of a circle, given that $A = \pi r^2$

Divide both sides by π to isolate the square term $\qquad \dfrac{A}{\pi} = r^2$

Take the square root each side $\qquad \sqrt{\dfrac{A}{\pi}} = r$

Turn the equation around to make r the subject $\qquad r = \sqrt{\dfrac{A}{\pi}}$

Practice Exercise

1 Match the sequences and the nth terms.
Find the nth term for the sequence left over.

5, 6, 7, 8, ...	4n
5, 8, 11, 14, ...	$n + 3$
4, 8, 12, 16, ...	$n + 4$
4, 5, 6, 7, ...	3$n + 2$
6, 12, 18, 24, ...	....

2 Find the nth term of the sequence

18, 15, 12, 9, ...

....

....

....

3 Use the signs $>$ or $<$ to complete the following:

(a)   5   3

(b) -2   4

(c) 3^2   6

(d)   0.25   ....   0.2

4 Complete the following to make x the subject of the formula.

$y = mx + c$

.... Subtract from both sides of the formula

.... Divide both sides of the formula by m

$x =$ .... Turn the formula around to make x the subject

Topic 9
More using algebra

Sequences using the method of differences

If the rule to obtain a sequence is not obvious to you, try the method of differences. The method of differences involves finding the difference between successive terms of the sequence.

Like this

To find the next two terms of the sequence 3, 8, 15, 24, 36, ..., draw a diagram to find the differences.

$$3, \quad 8, \quad 15, \quad 24, \quad 36, ...$$

$(+5)$ $+7$ $+9$ $+11$ First differences

$(+2)$ $+2$ $+2$ Second differences

The number $+5$ is called the first difference (of the set of first differences)

The number $+2$ is called the second difference (of the set of second differences)

As the second differences are all the same then

nth term = first term + 1st difference $\times (n-1)$ + 2nd difference $\times \frac{1}{2}(n-1)(n-2)$

Like this

Find the nth term of the sequence above.

$$n\text{th term} = \text{first term} + \text{1st difference} \times (n-1) + \text{2nd difference} \times \tfrac{1}{2}(n-1)(n-2)$$
$$= 3 + (n-1) \times 5 + \tfrac{1}{2}(n-1)(n-2) \times 2$$
$$= 3 + 5n - 5 + 1(n^2 - 3n + 2)$$
$$= n^2 + 2n$$

Inequalities

To solve inequalities you proceed in exactly the same way as you do with equalities (equations) except when you multiply or divide by a negative number. When you multiply or divide by a negative number you must change the direction of the inequality.

Note: To solve inequalities of the form $6 > x + 3 > -1$ you must write these as two separate inequalities (i.e. $6 > x + 3$ and $x + 3 > -1$) and then solve each part separately.

Like this

Solve $19 - 2x > 9$

Add $2x$ to each side $\quad 19 > 2x + 9$

Subtract 9 from each side $\quad 19 - 9 > 2x$

$\quad 10 > 2x$

Divide each side by 2 $\quad 5 > x \quad$ or $\quad x < 5$

Solving cubic equations

Cubic equations can be solved using a trial and improvement method.

Note: It is often useful to draw a sketch of the cubic graph to give you an idea of appropriate starting points for your first approximations.

Like this

Use trial and improvement to solve $x^3 - x^2 = 10$. Give your answer to 1 dp.

First find the two integer values between which the solution lies.

Try $x = 2 \quad 2^3 - 2^2 = 8 - 4 = 4 \quad$ too small

Try $x = 3 \quad 3^3 - 3^2 = 27 - 9 = 18 \quad$ too big $\quad$ so $2 < x < 3$

Then find the two values of 1 dp between which the solution lies.

Try $x = 2.6 \quad 2.6^3 - 2.6^2 = 17.576 - 6.76 = 10.816 \quad$ too big

Try $x = 2.5 \quad 2.5^3 - 2.5^2 = 15.625 - 6.25 = 9.375 \quad$ too small $\quad$ so $2.5 < x < 2.6$

To decide if the answer to 1 dp is 2.5 or 2.6 you must try 2.55.

Try $x = 2.55 \quad 2.55^3 - 2.55^2 = 16.581... - 6.5025 = 10.078... \quad$ too big

So $2.5 < x < 2.55$ and $x = 2.5$ (correct to 1 dp)

Practice Exercise

1 What is a correct algebraic description of the nth term of the sequence 2, 6, 12, 20, ...?

A $n^2 + n$ **C** $2n^2$

B $n^2 + 2$ **D** $n^2 + 1$

1 Answer ....

2 Use a table of differences to find the nth term of the sequence 3, 6, 11, 18, ...

....

....

....

....

3 Find a formula for the total number of rods in the nth pattern in this sequence:

....

4 Solve the following inequalities.

(a) $3x + 5 > 17$

....

(b) $4x + 3 \leqslant 3x + 9$

....

(c) $4(x + 4) > 2x + 21$

....

5 Which number line shows the solution to the inequality $-5 < 3x - 2 < 4$?

A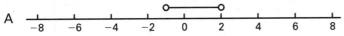

B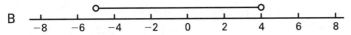

C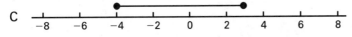

D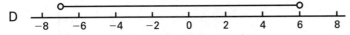

Topic 9
More using algebra

Summary

Transforming (or changing) the subject of formulae

When the term to be isolated appears on both sides of the equation you need to factorise.

Like this

Make y the subject in the following formula: $b(y - c) = y + a$

Get rid of the brackets $\qquad\qquad\qquad by - bc = y + a$

Collect the y terms on one side $\qquad\quad by - y = a + bc$

Factorise to isolate y $\qquad\qquad\qquad y(b - 1) = a + bc$

Divide both sides by $(b - 1)$ $\qquad\quad y = \dfrac{(a + bc)}{(b - 1)}$

Quadratic inequalities

You can solve quadratic inequalities by making a sketch of the graph.

Like this

(a) Solve $(x - 2)(x + 1) < 0$

You must first sketch the graph $y = (x - 2)(x + 1)$.

You want $y < 0$ that is 'the bit below' the x axis. This gives the solution $-1 < x < 2$

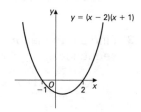

(b) Solve $x^2 - 2x - 15 > 0$

Before you sketch the graph you must factorise:
$x^2 - 2x - 15 = (x + 3)(x - 5)$
Now sketch $y = (x + 3)(x - 5)$

You want $y > 0$ that is 'the bit above' the x axis. This gives the solution $x < -3$ and $x > 5$

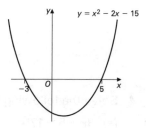

Solving cubic equations using graphs

Like this

Solve $x^3 - 7x + 6 = 0$ by plotting the graph of $y = x^3 - 7x + 6$ for $-4 < x < 3$.
To plot the graph make a table of values, plot corresponding x and y values and join these with a smooth curve.

x	-4	-3	-2	-1	0	1	2	3
x^3	-64	-27	-8	-1	0	1	8	27
$-7x$	28	21	14	7	0	-7	-14	-21
$+6$	6	6	6	6	6	6	6	6
y	-30	0	12	12	6	0	0	12

Where the graph cuts the x axis $y = 0$.

So these x values are the solutions of your equation: $x = -3$, $x = 1$ and $x = 2$.

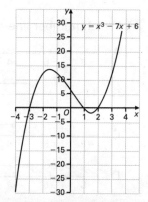

Practice Exercise

1 The equation of a graph is $y = \dfrac{x-2}{x-1}$

Express x in terms of y.

....

....

....

2 (a) Draw the graph of $y = x^2 + x - 6$ and explain how it can be used to solve the inequality $x^2 + x - 6 \leqslant 0$.

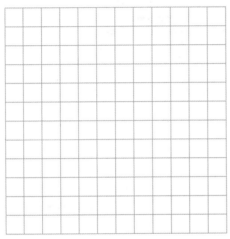

(b) Use your graph to estimate the solution to the inequality $x^2 + x - 6 \leqslant 2$.

....

3 Draw a graph of the equation $y = x^3 - 3x - 1$ for values of x from -3 to $+3$.

Use your graph to find estimates of the three solutions to the equation $x^3 - 3x - 1 = 0$.

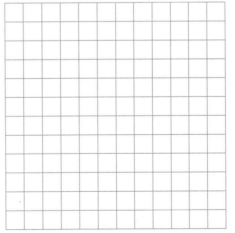

....

....

....

Use trial and improvement to find the smallest solution correct to 2 decimal places.

....

Algebra

Topic 9
More using algebra

Examination Questions

1. The first four terms in a sequence are 2, 8, 18, 32.

What is the next term in the sequence?

....

(SEG, Summer 1997 – Intermediate Paper 4)

2. Hexagons are used to make a sequence of patterns as shown.

  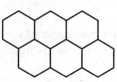

Pattern 1   **Pattern 2**   **Pattern 3**
10 outside edges   14 outside edges   18 outside edges

(a) How many outside edges has Pattern 8?

....

(b) Write down a rule to find the number of outside edges for Pattern *n*.

....

....

(SEG, Summer 1997 – Intermediate Paper 3)

Examination Questions

Topic 9
More using algebra

3. (a) Write down the *n*th term for each of the following sequences.

(i)   1, 4, 9, 16,

....

(ii) 4, 16, 36, 64,

....

(b) The *n*th term of another sequence is $(n + 1)(n + 2)$.
Explain why every term of the sequence is an even number.

....

....

(NEAB, Summer 1998 – Higher Paper 2H)

4. (a) What is the next number in this sequence?

1, 3, 7, 15, ...

(b) Find a formula, in terms of *n*, for the number of sticks in the *n*th shape in this sequence.

7 sticks   12 sticks   17 sticks

....

....

(c) Find a formula, in terms of *n*, for the *n*th term in this sequence.

2, 6, 12, 20, 30, ...

(SEG – specimen paper)

5. (a) The volume of a cone is given by the formula $V = \frac{1}{3}\pi r^2 h$. Rearrange the formula to give *r* in terms of *V* and *h*.

....

....

(SEG – specimen Higher Paper 15, part question)

Topic 9
More using algebra

Examination Questions

6. Solve the equation $x^3 = 22$ by trial and improvement.

   Start with $x = 2$.

   Give your final answer correct to **one** decimal place.

   You **must** show all your working.

   ....

   ....

   ....

   ....

   ....

   ....

   (SEG, Summer 1997 – Intermediate Paper 4)

7. Katy is using trial and improvement to find an answer to the question $x^3 - x = 35$.

   This table shows her first two tries.

x	$x^3 - x$	Comment
4	60	too big
3	24	too small

   Continue the table to find a solution to the equation.

x	$x^3 - x$	Comment
4	60	too big
3	24	too small

   Give your answer to **1 decimal place**

   ....

   (NEAB, Summer 1998 – Higher Paper)

8. (a) (i) Factorise fully the expression $2r^2 + 2rh$.

....

....

(ii) Multiply out $(2x + 3)(x - 4)$. Simplify your answer.

....

....

(b) A possible points system for the high jump event in athletics is given by

$P = a(M - b)^2$.

M is the height jumped in cm, P is the number of points awarded and a and b are non-zero positive constants.

(i) Zero points are scored for a height jumped of 75 cm. What is the value of the constant b?

....

....

(ii) Express M in terms of P, a, b.

....

....

(SEG – specimen paper)

9. Make p the subject of the formula

$$l = \frac{p - 6}{p + 2}$$

....

....

Topic 10
Angle properties

Angle properties

You need to know the following angle properties

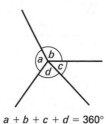

$a + b + c + d = 360°$
Angles in a full turn add up to 360°

$e + f = 180°$
Angles on a straight line add up to 180°

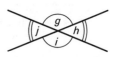

$g = i$ } two pairs of **vertically**
$j = k$ } **opposite** angles

Vertically opposite angles are equal

Angles in parallel lines

You need to know the following properties of angles in parallel lines

Note:

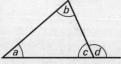

Angles r and s are also **alternate angles** or **Z angles**.

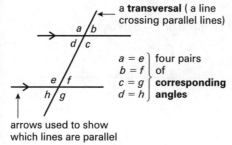

a **transversal** (a line crossing parallel lines)

arrows used to show which lines are parallel

$a = e$ } four pairs
$b = f$ } of
$c = g$ } **corresponding**
$d = h$ } **angles**

Corresponding angles are equal

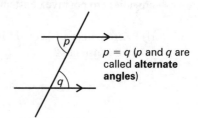

$p = q$ (p and q are called **alternate angles**)

Alternate angles between parallel lines are equal

Angles in triangles and quadrilaterals

The angle sum (or the sum of the angles) of a triangle is 180°

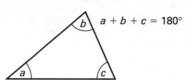

$a + b + c = 180°$

Note:

$d = a + b$ *(exterior angle = sum of interior opposite angles)*

The angle sum of a quadrilateral is 360°

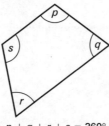

$p + q + r + s = 360°$

Practice Exercise

1 Find the missing angles.

(a)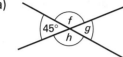

(b)

(c)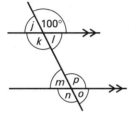

(d)

(e)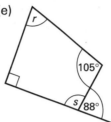

1 (a) Answer f = ...°

g = ...°

h = ...°

1 (b) Answer i = ...°

1 (c) Answer j = ...°

k = ...°

l = ...°

m = ...°

n = ...°

o = ...°

p = ...°

1 (d) Answer q = ...°

1 (e) Answer r = ...°

s = ...°

2 Match the statements with the reasons.

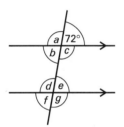

$a = 108°$	vertically opposite angles
$c = d$	corresponding angles
$b = 72°$	alternate angles
$e = 72°$	angles on a straight line

3 Say whether each of these statements (a)–(f) is true or false.

(a) The angles of a triangle add up to 90°

(b) The angles of a quadrilateral add up to 180°

(c) Opposite angles are equal

(d) Angles on a straight line are equal

(e) Alternate angles are equal

(f) Interior angles add up to 360°

3 (a) Answer ....

3 (b) Answer ....

3 (c) Answer ....

3 (d) Answer ....

3 (e) Answer ....

3 (f) Answer ....

4

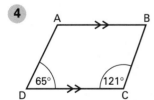

(a) Explain why line DA is not parallel to line CB.

....

....

(b) Find the sizes of the other two angles of the quadrilateral ABCD, stating any angle properties you use.

....

....

Shape, Space and Measures

Topic 10
Angle properties

Note: You should notice that for an n-sided polygon the angle sum is (n − 2) × 180°

Note: Work on angles in a semicircle will only be tested on the higher tier by NEAB.

Note: The property works 'the other way round' so that if XC bisects chord AXB at right angles then XC goes through O, and so is a radius.

Summary

Angle sums

The angle sum (or the sum of the angles) of shapes can be found by dividing them into triangles

Like this

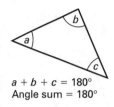

$a + b + c = 180°$
Angle sum = 180°

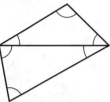

A quadrilateral can be split into two triangles

Angle sum = 2 × 180°
= 360°

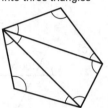

A pentagon can be split into three triangles

Angle sum = 3 × 180°
= 540°

Angle properties of circles

Angle in a semicircle is 90°.

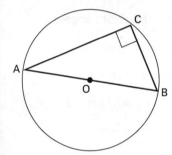

If AB is a diameter of the circle (i.e. passes through the centre) then angle ACB (written ∠ACB or AĈB) is 90°

Chords and radii

A radius which goes through the centre of a chord is perpendicular to the chord.

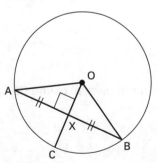

OC is a radius and cuts the chord AB at X such that AX = XB.
So radius OC is perpendicular to chord AXB.

Practice Exercise

1 Split these shapes into triangles and find their angle sum.

(a)

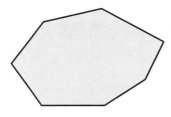

(b)

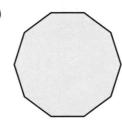

Angle sum = ...°

Angle sum = ...°

2 (a) Use the formula for the sum of angles of an *n*-sided polygon to show that the sum of the angles of a hexagon (a six-sided shape) is 720°.

....

....

(b) Show how you can get the same result by dividing a hexagon into triangles.

(c) What is the size of each angle of a **regular** hexagon?

....

....

3 Look at the diagram and then say whether each of the statements (a)–(e) is true or false.

(a) AE = EC

(b) *a* and *d* are 60°

(c) *p = a + d*

(d) *d = b*

(e) *c* is a right angle

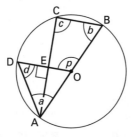

3 (a) Answer ....

3 (b) Answer ....

3 (c) Answer ....

3 (d) Answer ....

3 (e) Answer ....

(f) Write down another true statement about this diagram

....

97

Shape, Space and Measures

Topic 10
Angle properties

More angle properties of circles

1 Angles in the same segment are equal.

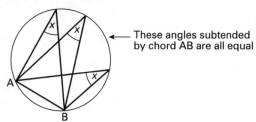

These angles subtended by chord AB are all equal

2 The angle at the centre equals twice the angle at the circumference.

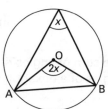

Angle subtended by chord AB at the centre = 2 × angle subtended by chord AB at the circumference

3 Opposite angles of a cyclic quadrilateral add up to 180°

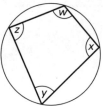

A cyclic quadrilateral has all four vertices (corners) on the circumference of a circle

$w + y = 180°$
$x + z = 180°$ } both pairs of opposite angles in a cyclic quadrilateral add up to 180°

4 The angle between the tangent and radius is 90°.

this angle is 90°

tangent to the circle

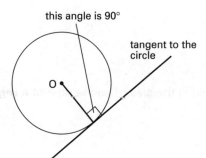

Note: A tangent is a straight line which touches a circle at a point.

5 Tangents from a point outside a circle are equal in length.

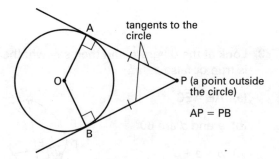

tangents to the circle

P (a point outside the circle)

AP = PB

Note: If O is the centre of the circle triangle AOP is congruent to triangle BOP.

6 The angle between the tangent and chord equals the angle in the alternate segment.

angle in the alternate segment

chord AB

tangent to the circle

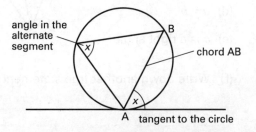

Practice Exercise

1 Find the missing angles.

(a)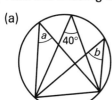

(b)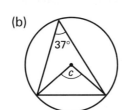

(c)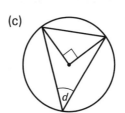

1 (a) Answer a = ...°

b = ...°

1 (b) Answer c = ...°

1 (c) Answer d = ...°

2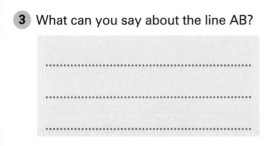

(a) What is the special name given to this quadrilateral?

....

(b) Find angle *a*.

2 (b) Answer a = ...°

3 What can you say about the line AB?

....

....

....

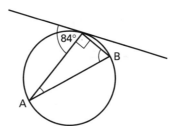

4 Complete the sentences (a)–(d).

(a) The angle subtended by a chord at the centre of a circle equals

....

(b) Opposite angles of a cyclic quadrilateral

....

(c) Tangents from a point outside a circle to the circle

....

(d) The angle between the tangent and chord equals

....

5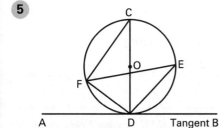

3 right angles are

..........., ... and ....

3 other equal angles are

..........., ... and ....

Topic 10
Angle
properties

Examination Questions

1. Find the sizes of the angles marked by the letters in these diagrams

(a)

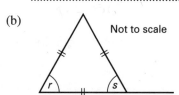

Not to scale

....

(b)

Not to scale

....

(c)

Not to scale

....

(NEAB – specimen paper)

2. AB is parallel to CD. CP = DP. Angle CPD = 110°.

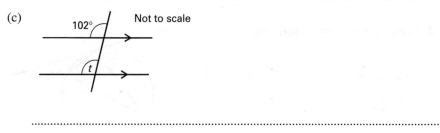

Not to scale

(a) (i) Which of the following correctly describes the angle CPD?

   right angle   acute angle   obtuse angle   reflex angle

   ....

(ii) Which of the following correctly describes the triangle CPD?

   right angled   isosceles   equilateral   scalene

   ....

(b) Work out the size of angle CDP.

....

(c) Write down the size of the angle BPD. Give a reason for your answer.

....

....

(SEG, Summer 1998 – Paper 11)

3. The diagram shows two straight lines AB and PQ which cross at O.

The line OT is perpendicular to AB.

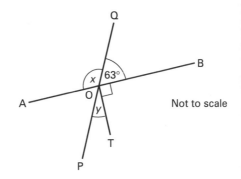

Not to scale

Angle BOT = 90°

Angle QOB = 63°

Work out the sizes of angle x and angle y.

....

....

$x =$ .... degrees

$y =$ .... degrees

(SEG, Winter 1998 – Paper 13)

4. The diagram shows a regular 12 sided polygon (called a dodecagon).
Each interior angle is 150°.

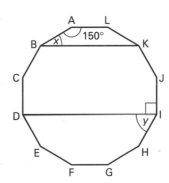

The lines BK and DI have been drawn.

(a) (i) What is the special name for the polygon ALKB?

....

(ii) Calculate the size of the angle marked x.

....

(b) Calculate the size of the angle marked y.

....

(c) Calculate the sum of the angles in the polygon DEFGHI.

....

....

(NEAB – specimen paper)

Topic 10
Angle properties

Examination Questions

5. The diagram shows a regular octagon with centre O.

(a) Work out the size of angle x.

....

....

.... degrees

(b) Work out the size of angle y.

....

....

.... degrees

(SEG, Summer 1998 – Paper 13)

6.

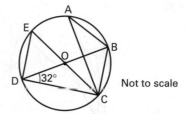

Not to scale

A, B, C, D and E are points on the circumference of a circle centre O. Angle BDC is 32°.

Write down the values of

(a) Angle CAB,

....

(b) Angle COB,

....

(c) Angle DCB,

....

(d) Angle DEC,

....

(NEAB – specimen paper)

Topic 10
Angle
properties

7. ABCD is a cyclic quadrilateral

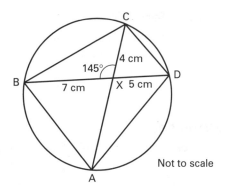

Not to scale

The diagonals AC and BD intersect at X.
BX = 7 cm, CX = 4 cm, DX = 5 cm and
angle CXB = 145°

(a) Explain why triangles BXC and AXD are similar.

....

....

....

(b) Calculate the length of AX

....

....

(SEG, Summer 1998 – Paper 15, part question)

8. TPK is a tangent to the circle
TSQ is a straight line
PQ = QR
∠QPK = 50°
∠STP = 26°

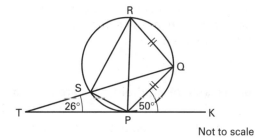

Not to scale

Calculate the size of

(a) angle PQR

....

....

(b) angle QRS

....

....

(NEAB – specimen paper)

Shape, Space and Measures

Topic 11
Length, area and volume

Note: Where you are allowed to use your calculator, it is best to use the $\boxed{\pi}$ key for your calculations.

Note: You must be able to use the circumference formula 'the other way round' so that if $C = \pi \times d$
then $d = \dfrac{C}{\pi}$

Note: You must be able to use the formula for the area of a circle 'the other way round' so that if $A = \pi r^2$ then $r = \sqrt{\dfrac{A}{\pi}}$

Summary

About length

Circumference is the special name for the perimeter of a circle.
Circumference of a circle $= \pi \times$ diameter
The circumference of this circle is $\pi \times d = \pi d$
π is a number which is approximately 3.142

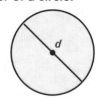

About area

Area of a triangle $=$ half $\times$ base $\times$ height

Area of all these triangles is $\frac{1}{2} \times b \times h = \frac{1}{2}bh$

Area of circle $= \pi \times$ (radius)^2
Area of this circle is $\pi \times r^2 = \pi r^2$

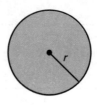

About surface area

This is the area of all the surfaces of a 3D shape. You could think of it as the 'skin area'.

Surface area of a cube $= 6 \times$ area of a face
This cube has 6 faces each of area $a \times a = a^2$
Surface area is $6a^2$

Surface area of a cuboid $= 2 \times$ area of top face $+ 2 \times$ area of front face
$\qquad\qquad\qquad\qquad\qquad\quad + 2 \times$ **area of side face**

For this cuboid: area of top face is $a \times b = ab$
$\qquad\qquad\qquad$ area of front face is $a \times c = ac$
$\qquad\qquad\qquad$ area of side face is $b \times c = bc$

Surface area is $2ab + 2ac + 2bc$
$\qquad\qquad\quad = 2(ab + ac + ab)$

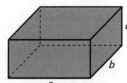

Practice Exercise

1 Which of these triangles have area 15 cm²?

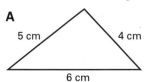

A

5 cm   4 cm

6 cm

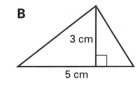

B

3 cm

5 cm

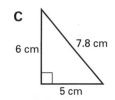

C

6 cm   7.8 cm

5 cm

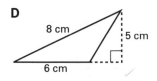

D

8 cm   5 cm

6 cm

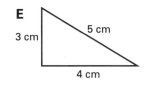

E

5 cm

3 cm

4 cm

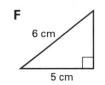

F

6 cm

5 cm

1 Answer ....

2 Complete the following information to find the area of this shape.

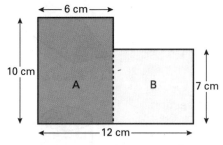

6 cm

10 cm

A

B

7 cm

12 cm

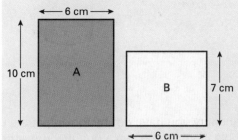

6 cm

10 cm   A

B   7 cm

6 cm

Area of A = ... = ...

Area of B = ... = ...

Total area = ... + ...

= .... cm²

3 Find the area of these shapes.

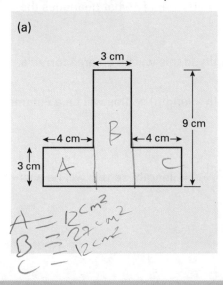

(a)

3 cm

9 cm

←4 cm→   B   ←4 cm→

3 cm   A   C

A = 12 cm²
B = 27 cm²   12 cm²
C = 12 cm²

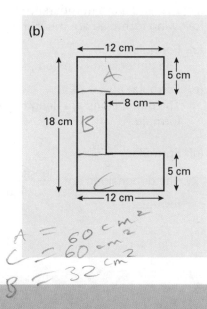

(b)

12 cm

5 cm

←8 cm→

18 cm   B

5 cm

12 cm

A = 60 cm²
C = 60 cm²
B = 32 cm²

3 (a) Answer 51 cm²

3 (b) Answer 152 cm²

105

Topic 11
Length, area
and volume

*Note: Because area
involves 2 dimensions
make sure that you
use the same units of
length for each.
Do not, for example,
mix metres and
centimetres.*

*Note: You may find it
useful to think of a
cylinder as a 'prism'
with a circular cross
section.*

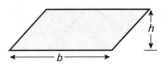

More about area

Area of parallelogram = base × height
Area of this parallelogram is $b \times h = bh$

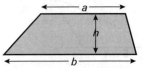

Area of a trapezium = half height × sum of parallel sides
Area of this trapezium is $\frac{1}{2} \times h \times (a + b) = \frac{1}{2}h(a + b)$

About volume

A **prism** is a shape with a constant polygonal cross section.
You can think of a Toblerone or 'T' bar.

Volume of a prism = area of cross section × length
Volume of this prism is $A \times l = Al$

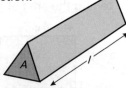

(A = area of cross section)

A **cylinder** is a shape with circular cross section.
You can think of a can of cola!

Volume of a cylinder = area of base × height
Volume of this cylinder is $\pi \times r^2 \times h = \pi r^2 h$

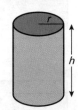

About dimensions

You can recognise what type of quantity you have got by looking at the units in which it is measured. For example, if you are given a quantity measured in m^2 you would know you are dealing with area.

Like this

If a, b, c and d are numbers for length units, identify what quantities the following formulae are measuring:

(a) Formula: $4\pi ab$
    The dimensions are [length × length] so this will be an area formula.

*Note: The dimension
of a [length + length] is
a [length] dimension.*

(b) Formula: $ab(c + d)$
    The dimensions are [length × length × length] so this will be a volume formula.

*Note: 4 and π are
numbers which don't
have units so don't
affect the dimensions.*

(c) Formula: $\dfrac{4\pi ab}{c}$
    The dimensions are $\left[\dfrac{\text{length} \times \text{length}}{\text{length}} \right]$ = [length] so this will be a length formula.

Practice Exercise

1 Complete the following:

Area of parallelogram = ...

Area of trapezium = ...

Volume of a cylinder = ...

2 Arrange these triangles, rectangles, parallelograms and trapeziums in ascending order of their areas.

A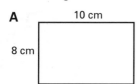

B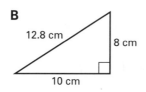

C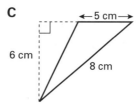

D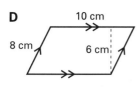

E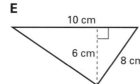

F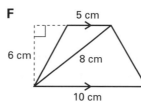

Smallest area ...., ..., ..., ..., ..., ... largest area

3 Work out the volume of the prisms in (a)–(d).

(a)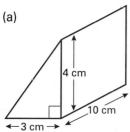

(b)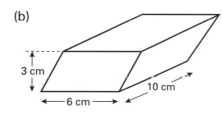

(c)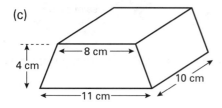

(d)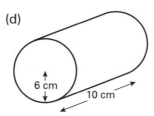

3 (a) Answer .... cm³

3 (b) Answer .... cm³

3 (c) Answer .... cm³

3 (d) Answer .... cm³

4 If a, b, and c are lengths, put these formulae into the correct sets

$$\pi a^2 \qquad a+b+c \qquad ab+ac \qquad abc \qquad a^2b$$
$$a^2+b^2 \qquad 2a+2b \qquad 4(a+b+c)$$

Lengths ....   Areas ....   Volumes ....

....

107

Topic 11
Length, area and volume

Note: Check whether the surface area of a cone should include the base in which case this should also be added on. Total surface area = curved surface area + area of base. For the cone in the diagram this is $\pi r l + \pi r^2$.

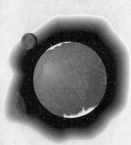

Summary

More about area and volume

A **cone** is a pyramid with a circular base. You can think of a traffic cone.

Curved surface area of cone = $\pi \times$ radius $\times$ slant height
Curved surface area of this cone is $\pi \times r \times l = \pi r l$

Volume of a cone is $\frac{1}{3} \times$ area of base $\times$ height
Volume of this cone is $\frac{1}{3} \times \pi r^2 \times h = \frac{1}{3}\pi r^2 h$

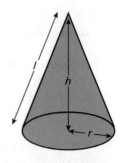

Think of all those frozen peas as **spheres**!
Surface area of sphere is $4 \times \pi \times$ (radius)^2
Volume of a sphere is $\frac{4}{3} \times \pi \times$ (radius)^3

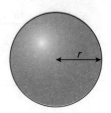

About arcs and sectors

Length of an arc of a circle with angle θ at the centre is $\frac{\theta}{360} \times$ circumference

Length of this arc is $\frac{\theta}{360} \times 2\pi r$

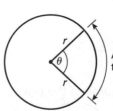

Arc length (part of the circumference)

Area of a sector of a circle with angle θ at the centre is $\frac{\theta}{360} \times$ area of circle

Area of this sector is $\frac{\theta}{360} \times \pi r^2$

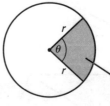

Area of sector (part of the area of the circle)

If you can't find an area directly then you should divide it into shapes you can do!

Like this
Find the area of the shaded part.

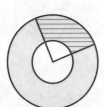

Shaded area = area of large sector − area of small sector

Practice Exercise

1 Work out (i) the total surface area and (ii) the volume of the solids below.

(a)

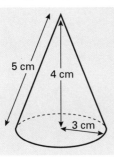

Surface area (without base) ....

Surface area (with base) ....

Volume ....

....

(b)

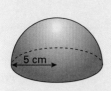

Surface area (without base)...........................

Surface area (with base) ....

Volume ....

....

2 Find the arc length and sector area for each of the following.

(a)

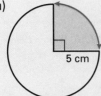

Arc length ....

....

Sector area ....

....

(b)

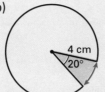

Arc length ....

....

Sector area ....

....

(c)

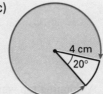

Arc length ....

....

Sector area ....

....

Find the area of the shaded regions.

3

(a)

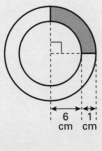

Area ....

....

(b)

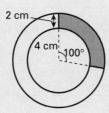

Area ....

....

Shape, Space and Measures

Topic 11

Length, area and volume

Examination Questions

1. The dimensions of a metal waste bin are 30 cm by 10 cm by 40 cm.

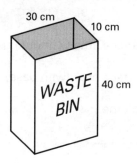

Calculate the volume of the bin, stating your units

....

....

(SEG – specimen paper)

2. Calculate the area of a circle with a diameter of 15 cm.
Give your answer to an appropriate degree of accuracy.

....

....

(NEAB, Winter 1998 – Paper 1)

3. A spinning top which consists of a cone of base radius 5 cm, height 9 cm and a hemisphere of radius 5 cm is illustrated.

9 cm

5 cm

(a) Calculate the volume of the spinning top.

....

....

(b) Calculate the total surface area of the spinning top.

....

....

....

(SEG – specimen paper)

Examination Questions

4. (a) A circle has a diameter of 7 cm.

   (i) Calculate the circumference of this circle.

   ....

   ....

   (ii) Calculate the area of this circle.

   ....

   ....

(b) A plastic beaker has a height of 10 cm and a circular base of diameter 7 cm.

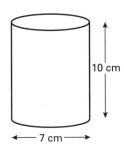

Calculate the volume of the beaker.

....

....

....

(NEAB, Summer 1997 – Paper 2)

5.

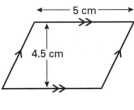

Shape A

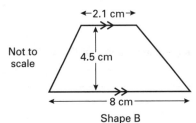

Not to scale

Shape B

Which of these shapes has the larger area?

You must show all your working clearly.

....

....

....

(NEAB – specimen paper)

Topic 11

Length, area and volume

6. The cylinder is 20 cm high and holds 1000 cm³ of water.

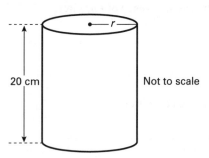

20 cm

Not to scale

Find the radius of the cylinder.

....

....

....

....

(SEG, Summer 1998 – Paper 14)

7. Ice cream is sold in a box that is the shape of a prism.
The ends are parallelograms.
The size of the prism is shown in the diagram.
The length of the prism is 12 cm.

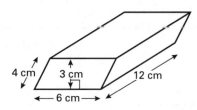

4 cm 3 cm 12 cm

← 6 cm →

Calculate the volume of the ice cream in the box.

....

....

....

....

....

(NEAB, Summer 1998 – Paper 2)

Topic 11

Length, area and volume

8. An equilateral triangle, ABC, is drawn inside a circle of radius 5 cm, as shown.

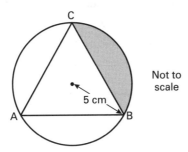

Not to scale

5 cm

(a) Calculate the length of AB.

Give your answer correct to 1 decimal place.

....

....

....

....

(b) Calculate the shaded area.

Give your answer correct to 1 decimal place.

....

....

....

....

(NEAB, Winter 1997 – Paper 1)

Topic 11
Length, area
and volume

Examination Questions

8. The diagram represents the cross section of a road tunnel.

The width of the road is 7 m and the side walls are 3.5 m high.

The roof is an arc of a circle centre O.

Calculate the area of the cross-section of the tunnel.

(Remember to state the units in your answer)

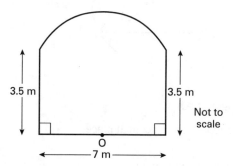

....

....

....

....

....

....

(NEAB – specimen paper)

Examination Questions

10. A minor sector AOB is cut from a circle of radius 20 cm. Angle AOB = 45°.

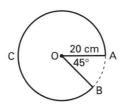

(a) Calculate the length of the arc ACB.

....

....

....

The radii OA and OB are joined without overlap so that a cone is formed, as shown in the diagram.

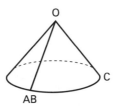

(b) Calculate
   (i) the base radius of the cone,

....

....

....

   (ii) the volume of the cone,

....

....

....

....

....

....

(NEAB, Summer 1998 – Paper 1)

Shape, Space and Measures

Topic 12

Symmetry and transformations

Note: You could check your reflection is correct by folding along the given line, using tracing paper or using a mirror.

Note: You could check your rotation is correct by using tracing paper.

Summary

Plane symmetry

A plane of symmetry divides a solid into two equal halves. Should look like:

Like this

Reflection

You must be able to reflect a figure in a given line.

Like this

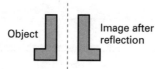

Rotation

You must be able to rotate a figure through $\frac{1}{4}$, $\frac{1}{2}$, or $\frac{3}{4}$ turns about a given point. (called the centre of rotation)

Like this

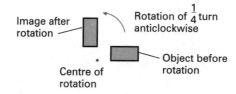

Enlargement

Enlargement with positive scale factor.

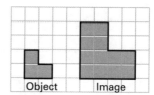

Here the enlargement has scale factor 2 (or all of the lengths are multiplied by 2)

Translation

A translation can be defined as a movement to the right (or the left) followed by a movement upwards (or downwards)

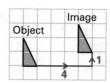

Here the shape has moved 4 units to the right followed by 1 unit up

Tessellations

If shapes fit together without any gaps then they are said to tessellate.

Shapes which tessellate

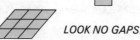 *LOOK NO GAPS!*

Shapes which do not tessellate

GAPS!

Practice Exercise

1 How many planes of symmetry do the following solids have?

(a)   (b) 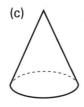 (c) 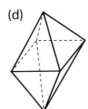 (d)

1 (a) Answer ....

1 (b) Answer ....

1 (c) Answer ....

1 (d) Answer ....

2 The diagram shows an L-shaped solid standing on a mirror.
Draw the reflection of the solid in the mirror.

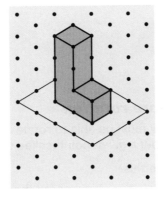

3

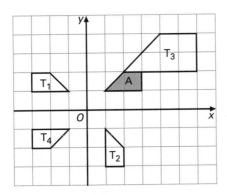

(a) Which shape is a rotation of A of $\frac{1}{4}$ turn clockwise about (0, 0)?

(b) Which shape is an enlargement of A with scale factor 2, centre (0, 0)?

(c) Which shape is a reflection of A in the y axis?

(d) Which shape is a rotation of A of $\frac{1}{2}$ turn about (0, 0)?

(e) On the same axes draw and label T_5, the reflection of A in the x axis.

3 (a) Answer ....

3 (b) Answer ....

3 (c) Answer ....

3 (d) Answer ....

4 Here is a trapezium with the mid-point of each side marked.
Rotate the trapezium 180° about each mid-point and draw its new positions.
Rotate the new trapeziums again and hence make a tessellation covering the dotted paper.

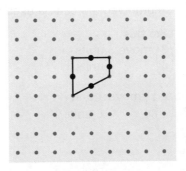

Shape, Space and Measures

Topic 12
Symmetry and transformations

Note: Once again, you could check your reflection by folding along the given line, using tracing paper or using a mirror.

Note: Once again, you could check your rotation is correct by using tracing paper.

Note: A fractional scale factor (less than 1) makes the shape smaller.

Note: Work on column vectors will only be tested on the higher tier by NEAB.

Summary

More reflection

You must be able to reflect a figure in a given line including the lines $y = x$ and $y = -x$.

Like this

Reflect the object in the line $y = x$

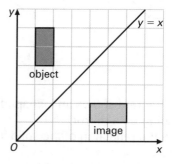

More rotation

You must be able to rotate a figure through any angle in a given direction about a given point (called the centre of rotation).

Like this

Rotate the object about the origin through 90° in a clockwise direction.

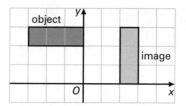

More enlargement

Enlargement with fractional scale factor (SF).

The enlargement of A to B is SF 3

The enlargement of B to A is SF $\frac{1}{3}$

(i.e. lengths in A are one-third those in B)

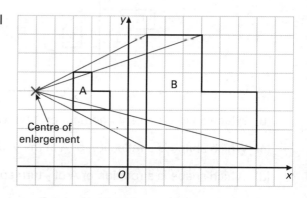

More translation

Column vectors can be used to specify translations.

Like this

$\begin{pmatrix} 3 \\ 4 \end{pmatrix}$ move 3 units → 4 units ↑

$\begin{pmatrix} 2 \\ -5 \end{pmatrix}$ move 2 units → 5 units ↓

$\begin{pmatrix} -1 \\ 6 \end{pmatrix}$ move 1 unit ← 6 units ↑

$\begin{pmatrix} -5 \\ -8 \end{pmatrix}$ move 5 units ← 8 units ↓

Practice Exercise

1

(a) Draw T₁, the reflection of A in the line $y = x$.

(b) Draw T₂, the rotation of T₁ 90° anticlockwise about (0, 0).

(c) What **single** transformation would transform A onto T₂?

....

(d)

T₃ is an enlargement of A with scale factor ....

centre (..........., ...).

(e)

The co-ordinates of A after a translation with vector $\begin{pmatrix} 3 \\ 2 \end{pmatrix}$ are

(..........., ...), (..........., ...) and (..........., ...).

2 This is part of a tessellation of octagons and squares.

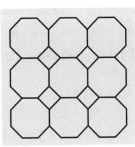

(a) On the diagram, mark:

    (i) a line of symmetry

    (ii) a point, A, about which there is rotational symmetry of order 4

    (iii) a point, D, about which there is rotational symmetry of order 2.

(b) Use the diagram to explain why each angle of a regular octagon is 135°.

....

....

Shape, Space and Measures

Topic 12

Symmetry and transformations

Summary

Even more enlargement

Enlargement with negative scale factor (SF).

A negative enlargement enlarges the shape 'backwards' through the centre of enlargement.

The enlargement A to B is SF -2

The enlargement B to A is SF $-\frac{1}{2}$

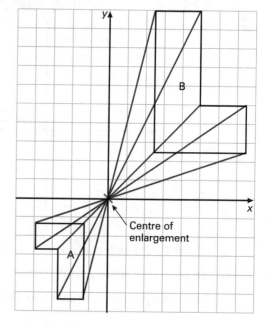

Centre of enlargement

Vectors and geometry

Vectors can be added, subtracted or multiplied by a constant.

Like this

If $\mathbf{a} = \begin{pmatrix} 1 \\ 2 \end{pmatrix}$ and $\mathbf{b} = \begin{pmatrix} 2 \\ -3 \end{pmatrix}$ then:

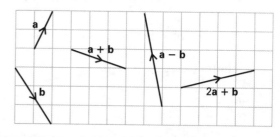

$$\mathbf{a} + \mathbf{b} = \begin{pmatrix} 1 \\ 2 \end{pmatrix} + \begin{pmatrix} 2 \\ -3 \end{pmatrix} = \begin{pmatrix} 3 \\ -1 \end{pmatrix}$$

$$\mathbf{a} - \mathbf{b} = \begin{pmatrix} 1 \\ 2 \end{pmatrix} - \begin{pmatrix} 2 \\ -3 \end{pmatrix} = \begin{pmatrix} -1 \\ 5 \end{pmatrix}$$

$$2\mathbf{a} + \mathbf{b} = 2 \times \begin{pmatrix} 1 \\ 2 \end{pmatrix} + \begin{pmatrix} 2 \\ -3 \end{pmatrix} = \begin{pmatrix} 4 \\ 1 \end{pmatrix}$$

Vectors can also be useful in geometry

Like this

ABCD is a parallelogram in which $\overrightarrow{AB} = 3\mathbf{p} + 4\mathbf{q}$, $\overrightarrow{AD} = \mathbf{p} - 2\mathbf{q}$ and $\overrightarrow{DO} = \mathbf{p} + 3\mathbf{q}$

Find $\overrightarrow{AC}$ and show that O is the mid point of AC.

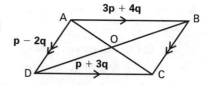

$$\begin{aligned} \overrightarrow{AC} &= \overrightarrow{AD} + \overrightarrow{DC} \\ &= \overrightarrow{AD} + \overrightarrow{AB} \qquad \text{(as } \overrightarrow{DC} \text{ and } \overrightarrow{AB} \text{ are equal vectors)} \\ &= (\mathbf{p} - 2\mathbf{q}) + (3\mathbf{p} + 4\mathbf{q}) \\ &= 4\mathbf{p} + 2\mathbf{q} \\ &= 2(2\mathbf{p} + \mathbf{q}) \end{aligned}$$

To show that O is the mid-point of AC you must show that $\overrightarrow{AC} = 2\overrightarrow{AO}$.

$$\begin{aligned} \overrightarrow{AO} &= \overrightarrow{AD} + \overrightarrow{DO} \\ &= (\mathbf{p} - 2\mathbf{q}) + (\mathbf{p} + 3\mathbf{q}) \\ &= 2\mathbf{p} + \mathbf{q} \end{aligned}$$

$\overrightarrow{AC} = 2\overrightarrow{AO}$ so O must be the mid point of AC.

Practice Exercise

1

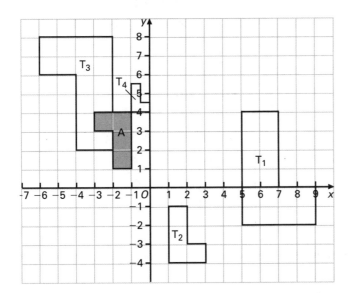

(a) Which shape is an enlargement of A with scale factor 2 centre (0, 0)?

1 (a) Answer ....

(b) Which shape is an enlargement of A with scale factor $-\frac{1}{2}$ centre (−1, 4)?

1 (b) Answer ....

(c) Which shape is an enlargement of A with scale factor −1 centre (0, 0)?

1 (c) Answer ....

(d) Which shape is an enlargement of A with scale factor −2 centre (1, 2)?

1 (d) Answer ....

2

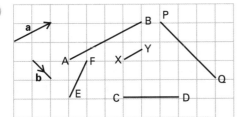

Match the vectors.

$\overrightarrow{AB}$	3**b**
$\overrightarrow{PQ}$	**a** − **b**
$\overrightarrow{BA}$	$\frac{1}{2}$**a**
$\overrightarrow{EF}$	**a** + **b**
$\overrightarrow{CD}$	−2**a**
$\overrightarrow{XY}$	2**a**

3

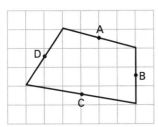

A, B, C and D are the mid-points of the sides of the quadrilateral.

Use vectors to show that ABCD is a parallelogram.

Examination Questions

1.

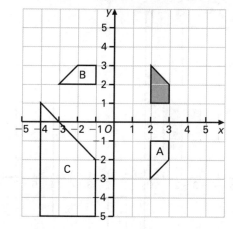

Describe fully a single transformation that would map the shaded shape on to

(a) shape A,

....

....

(b) shape B,

....

....

(c) shape C.

....

....

(NEAB, Summer 1997 – Paper 1)

2. (a) The diagram shows part of a wallpaper pattern.

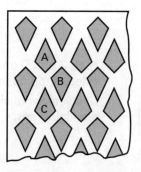

Using only one of the words, 'rotation, reflection or translation', describe the **single** transformation which maps:

(i)   the shape A onto the shape B;   ....

(ii) the shape A onto the shape C.   ....

Shape, Space
and Measures

Topic 12

Symmetry and
transformations

Intermediate Tier Only

Intermediate and Higher Tiers

Examination Questions

(b) Draw an enlargement of the kite with centre P and scale factor 3.

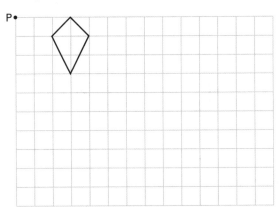

(SEG – specimen paper)

3. The diagram shows a triangle T.

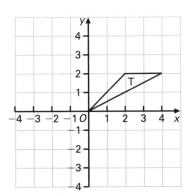

(a) Triangle A is obtained by rotating triangle T through 90° clockwise about O.
    Draw and label triangle A on the diagram.

(b) Triangle B is obtained by reflecting triangle T in the *y* axis.
    Draw and label triangle B on the diagram.

(c) Triangles T, A and B form part of a pattern which has line symmetry.

   (i) Draw and label the triangle C which will complete the pattern.

   (ii) How many lines of symmetry has the complete pattern?

   ....

(SEG – specimen paper)

Examination Questions

4. Triangle ABC and vectors **a** and **b** are shown on the grid.

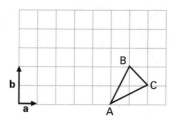

(a) Draw the position of the triangle ABC after translation by the vector **b** − 2**a**

(b) (i) Write the vector $\overrightarrow{AB}$ in terms of **a** and **b** ....

    (ii) Write the vector $\overrightarrow{BC}$ in terms of **a** and **b** ....

(c) D is an unmarked point on the grid.

$$\overrightarrow{BD} = \tfrac{2}{3}\overrightarrow{BC}$$
$$\overrightarrow{AD} = x\mathbf{a} + y\mathbf{b}$$

Use your answer to (b) to **calculate** the values of x and y.
You **must** show all your working

....

....

....

....

Answer $x =$ .... $y =$ ....

(SEG, Summer 1998 – Paper 16)

5.

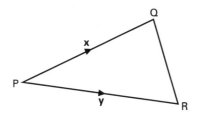

(a) Write down, in terms of **x** and **y**, the vector RQ

....

....

....

(b) The vectors $\overrightarrow{LM} = \mathbf{a} + 2\mathbf{b}$ and $\overrightarrow{LN} = \mathbf{a} - \mathbf{b}$ are drawn on the grid.

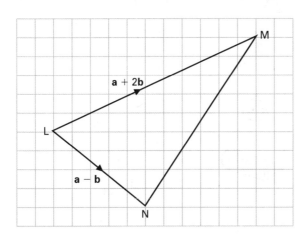

(i) Write down, in terms of **b**, the Vector $\overrightarrow{NM}$.

....

....

(ii) Hence find **b** in the form $\begin{pmatrix} p \\ q \end{pmatrix}$, where p and q are whole numbers.

....

....

(iii) Find **a** in the form $\begin{pmatrix} r \\ s \end{pmatrix}$, where r and s are whole numbers.

....

....

(NEAB, Winter 1997 – Paper 2)

Topic 13
Shapes and solids

Summary

Nets

Remember that a net is the shape you get if you cut open a 3D shape and flatten it out.

Name	Shape	Net	Number of faces	Number of vertices	Number of edges
Cube			6	8	12
Cuboid			6	8	12
Triangular prism			5	6	9
Triangular-based pyramid			4	4	6
Square-based pyramid			5	5	8
Cylinder			3	0	2

Isometric paper

You need to be able to draw 3D shapes on isometric paper.

Like this

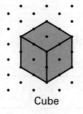

Cube

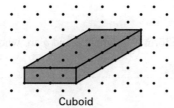

Cuboid

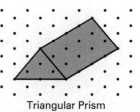

Triangular Prism

Practice Exercise

1 Match the nets with the shapes. Give the name of each of the shapes.

(a)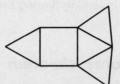

(b)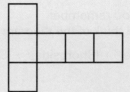

(c)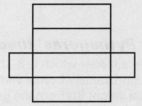

(d)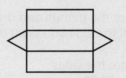

1 (a) Answer

....

1 (b) Answer

....

1 (c) Answer

....

1 (d) Answer

....

2 (a) Complete the following table.

Name of shape	No. of faces	No. of vertices	No. of edges
Cube	6	8	12
Cuboid			
Triangular prism			
Triangular pyramid			
Square pyramid			

(b) (i) What relationship do you notice between the number of faces, the number of vertices and the number of edges?

....

....

(ii) Does this always work?

....

Topic 13
Shapes and
solids

Note: *To show that a triangle is right-angled show that Pythagoras' theorem works!*

Summary

Working with right-angled triangles

Pythagoras' Theorem is used when you have a right-angled triangle and problems involving finding the lengths of the sides of the triangle.

Pythagoras' theorem

This states:
$c^2 = a^2 + b^2$

To help you remember
you could think of the theorem like this:

(Long side)^2 = (Short side)^2 + (Short side)^2

and

(Short side)^2 = (Long side)^2 − (Short side)^2

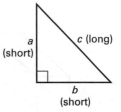

Using Pythagoras' theorem

You have a ladder which is 8.3 ft long. The ladder cannot be placed nearer than 3 ft horizontally from a vertical wall. Juliet is stuck upstairs at a window of vertical height 8 ft from the ground. If you were Romeo could you rescue her with the ladder?

1   Ignore the gumph and draw the correct right-angled triangle.
    Label the side you want (height you can reach with your ladder) 'x ft'

2   Square the sides:
    $8.3^2 = 68.89$
    $3^2 = 9$

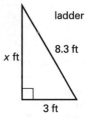

3   You want a short side so subtract.
    $x^2 = 8.3^2 - 3^2$
    $= 68.89 - 9$
    $= 59.89$

4   Find the square root to get x.
    $x = \sqrt{59.89} = 7.738\,863$
    As the window is 8 ft high then the answer is no, so bad luck Romeo!

Practice Exercise

 1

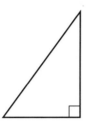

Measure the sides of the triangle.
Show that Pythagoras' theorem works for this triangle.

....

....

2 Find the missing lengths.

(a)

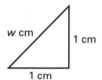
w cm   1 cm
1 cm

....

....

(b)

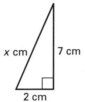
x cm   7 cm
2 cm

....

....

(c)

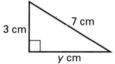
3 cm   7 cm
y cm

....

....

(d)

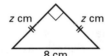
z cm z cm
8 cm

....

....

3 Use Pythagoras' theorem to find the height of this equilateral triangle.

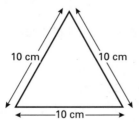
10 cm   10 cm
10 cm

....

....

....

Topic 13
Shapes and solids

Summary

Working in 3D

To work in 3D you 'pull out' the appropriate triangle from the 3D figure and draw the true shaped triangle.

You must be able to find the angle that a line, say AB, makes with a plane. To find this angle you first draw the perpendicular from the end of the line (B) to meet the plane at N. Then join AN.

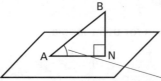

The angle that the line AB makes with the plane is B$\hat{A}$N or $\angle$BAN.

Like this

The diagram shows a pyramid with vertex P.

The square base QRST has sides 10 cm.

The edges PQ, PR, PS, PT are each 12 cm.

The centre of the base is M.

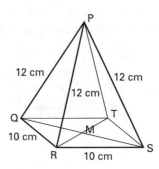

By making sketches of the appropriate right-angled triangles to assist you:

(a) Calculate the length of QS
    Pull out triangle QRS and use Pythagoras.

$QS^2 = QR^2 + RS^2$
$\quad\ = (10^2 + 10^2)\ cm^2$
$QS\ = \sqrt{200}\ cm$
$\quad\ = 14.142\,136\ cm$
$\quad\ = 14.1\ cm\ (3\ sf)$

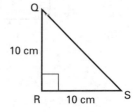

(b) Calculate the length of PM
    Pull out triangle PQM and use Pythagoras.

$QM = QS \div 2$
$\quad\quad = 14.142\,136\ cm \div 2 = 7.071\,068\ cm$

$PQ^2 = QM^2 + PM^2$
$12^2\ cm^2 = 7.071\,068^2\ cm^2 + PM^2$
$PM^2 = (12^2 - 7.071\,068^2)\ cm^2$
$PM = \sqrt{93.999\,997}\ cm$
$\quad\quad = 9.695\,359\,6\ cm$
$\quad\quad = 9.70\ cm\ (3\ sf)$

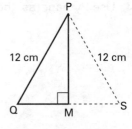

Note: Without rounding errors PM = $\sqrt{94}$. You should always try to work as accurately as possible.

Practice Exercise

1 Find the lengths of the diagonals AB, CD and EF of these cubes.

(a)   (b) 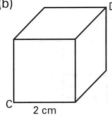   (c)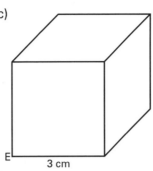

(a) ....

....

(b) ....

....

(c) ....

....

2 Find the volume of this square-based pyramid.

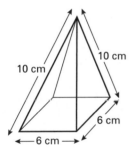

....

....

....

....

....

....

3 A cuboid measures 30 cm by 20 cm by 10 cm. Find the length of the diagonal of the cuboid.

....

....

....

....

....

Topic 13
Shapes and
solids

Examination Questions

1. The diagram shows a net of a cuboid

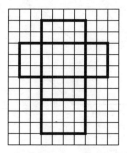

Use the grid below to show what the cuboid looks like when the net is folded.

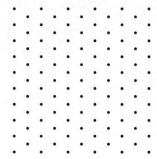

(SEG, Summer 1998 – Paper 12)

2. (a) Sketch a cube.

(b) Which **two** of these shapes are nets for a cube?

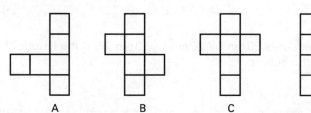

(NEAB, Summer 1997 – Paper 2)

3.

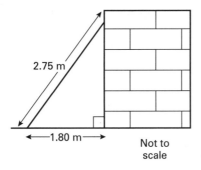

2.75 m

1.80 m

Not to scale

A ladder, 2.75 m long, leans against a wall.
The bottom of the ladder is 1.80 m from the wall on level ground.

Calculate how far the ladder reaches up the wall.
Give your answer to an appropriate degree of accuracy.

....

....

....

....

(NEAB, Summer 1998 – Paper 2)

4.   The diagram shows a semicircle and a right-angled triangle

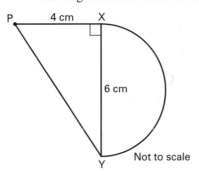

P   4 cm   X

6 cm

Y   Not to scale

(a) (i)   The semicircle has a radius of 3 cm.
            Calculate the area of the semicircle.

            ....

            ....

     (ii) The triangle is right angled at X.
            PX = 4 cm and XY = 6 cm.
            Calculate the length of PY.
            You **must** show all your working.

            ....

            ....

            ....

                                    (SEG, Winter 1998 – Paper 14)

Topic 13

Shapes and solids

Examination Questions

5. The diagram shows a cross section through a roof on a barn.

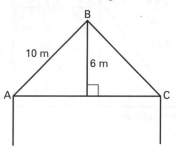

(a) Calculate
    (i) the length AC

....

....

....

    (ii) the area of triangle ABC

....

....

The building is 25 metres long.

(b) Calculate the volume of the roof space.

....

....

6. Jane designs a ramp for wheelchair users.
This is its cross-sectional view.

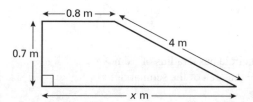

(a) Calculate the distance marked x m.
    Give your answer to 1 decimal place.

....

....

Shape, Space
and Measures

Topic 13

Shapes and
solids

Intermediate and Higher Tiers

Higher Tier only

Examination Questions

(b) The width of the ramp is 1.5 metres.

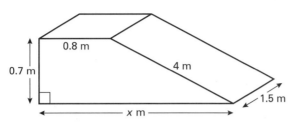

What volume of concrete is needed to build the ramp?

....

....

....

(NEAB – specimen paper)

7.

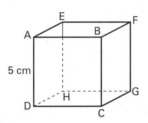

The diagram shows a cube of side 5 cm.
Calculate the following lengths leaving your answers in surd form.

(a) AC,

....

....

....

(b) AG.

....

....

....

Summary

About similar triangles

Similar triangles have equal angles (and their sides are in corresponding ratio).

 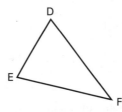

In the given triangles ABC and DEF,

$\angle ABC = \angle DEF$
$\angle BCA = \angle EFD$
$\angle CAB = \angle FDE$

so the triangles are similar.

Similarly, for similar triangles $\dfrac{AB}{DE} = \dfrac{BC}{EF} = \dfrac{AC}{DF}$.

About congruent triangles

Congruent triangles have equal angles and equal sides (i.e. they fit exactly over one another). In the case of triangles, there are 4 different sets of conditions which give congruent triangles.

1   All the **S**ides of one triangle equal all the **S**ides of the other triangle.
Remember **SSS** (side, side, side).

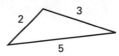   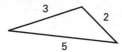

2   Two **S**ides and the **A**ngle between these sides of one triangle equal two **S**ides and the **A**ngle between these sides of the other triangle.
Remember **SAS** (side, angle, side).

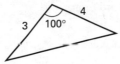   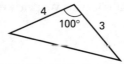

3   Two **A**ngles and one **S**ide of one triangle equal two **A**ngles and the corresponding **S**ide of the other triangle.
Remember **AAS** (angle, angle, corresponding side).

   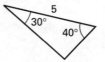

4   Each triangle is **R**ight angled. The **H**ypotenuse and one of the other **S**ides are equal.
Remember **RHS** (right angle, hypotenuse, side).

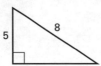   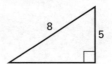

Practice Exercise

1 Use a ruler and protractor to make accurate scale drawings of the shapes (a)–(c)

(a)

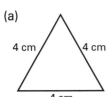

4 cm 4 cm

4 cm

(b)

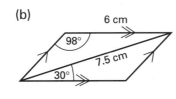

6 cm

98°

7.5 cm

30°

(c)

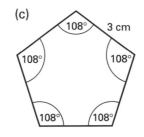

108° 3 cm

108°   108°

108°   108°

2 Say whether each pair of triangles is congruent and state the congruence condition you used.

(a)

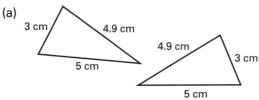

3 cm   4.9 cm

4.9 cm

5 cm   3 cm

5 cm

....

....

(b)

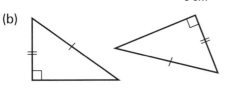

....

....

(c)

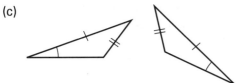

....

....

3 Make the links:

Two triangles with the same angles as each other	must be congruent
Two triangles with the same length sides as each other	could be congruent
Two triangles with the same perimeter but different areas	cannot be congruent

4 In the diagram AB is parallel to CD. AB = OC = 15 cm. OB = 12 cm.

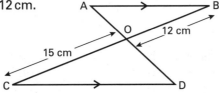

15 cm

A   B

O   12 cm

Not to scale

15 cm

C   D

Calculate the length of CD.

....

....

Shape, Space and Measures

Topic 14
Triangles and quadrilaterals

Working with trig ratios

The trig (short for trigonometric) ratios are defined like this:

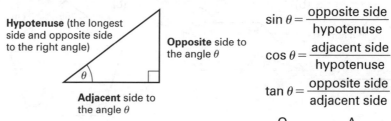

$$\sin \theta = \frac{\text{opposite side}}{\text{hypotenuse}}$$

$$\cos \theta = \frac{\text{adjacent side}}{\text{hypotenuse}}$$

$$\tan \theta = \frac{\text{opposite side}}{\text{adjacent side}}$$

Remember
$$S = \frac{O}{H} \qquad C = \frac{A}{H} \qquad T = \frac{O}{A}$$
or SOH $\qquad$ CAH $\qquad$ TOA

Finding the length of a side given one side and one angle

Find x in the figure below.

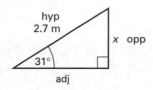

1 Label sides opp, adj and hyp.	opp $= x$, hyp $= 2.7$
2 Select the correct trig ratio.	you want opp and you have hyp so select sin
3 Find the value of the selected trig ratio.	$\sin 31° = 0.515\,038\,1$
4 Use the trig ratio to make an equation.	$\sin 31° = \dfrac{\text{opp}}{\text{adj}} = \dfrac{x}{2.7}$
5 Solve the equation.	$0.515\,038\,1 = \dfrac{x}{2.7}$
	$x = 2.7 \times 0.515\,038\,1 = 1.39\,\text{m (3 sf)}$

Finding the size of an angle given two sides

Find the angle z in the figure below.

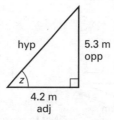

1 Label sides opp, adj and hyp.	opp $= 5.3$, adj $= 4.2$
2 Select the correct trig ratio.	You have opp and adj so select tan
3 Use the trig ratio to make an equation.	$\tan z = \dfrac{\text{opp}}{\text{adj}} = \dfrac{5.3}{4.2}$
	$\tan z = 1.261\,904\,8$
4 Use inverse tan to find the angle.	$z = 51.6° \text{ (3 sf)}$

Note: *Before you use any trig ratios make sure that your calculator is operating in degrees.*

Practice Exercise

1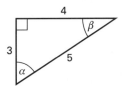

Say whether the following statements (a)–(f) are true or false.

(a) $\tan \alpha = \frac{3}{4}$

(b) $\cos \alpha = \frac{3}{5}$

(c) $\sin \alpha = \frac{4}{3}$

(d) $\tan \beta = \frac{3}{4}$

(e) $\cos \beta = \frac{4}{5}$

(f) $\sin \beta = \frac{4}{5}$

1 (a) Answer ....

1 (b) Answer ....

1 (c) Answer ....

1 (d) Answer ....

1 (e) Answer ....

1 (f) Answer ....

2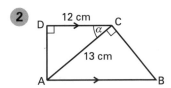

Find:

(a) AD ....

(b) $\cos \alpha$ ....

(c) AB ....

(d) BC ....

3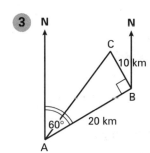

Explain why the bearing of A from B is 240°

....

....

What is the distance of C from A?

....

....

What is the bearing of C from A?

....

....

Shape, Space and Measures

Topic 14
Triangles and quadrilaterals

Note: Use small letters for sides, capitals for angles and remember that side and opposite angle go together.

Summary

Working with the sine rule

If you have a problem involving 2 sides and 2 angles of a non-right-angled triangle then you can use the **sine rule**.

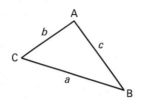

Use $\dfrac{a}{\sin A} = \dfrac{b}{\sin B} = \dfrac{c}{\sin C}$

when you want to find a side.

Use $\dfrac{\sin A}{a} = \dfrac{\sin B}{b} = \dfrac{\sin C}{c}$

when you want to find an angle.

Area of a triangle

This is a quick way to find the area of a non-right-angled triangle.

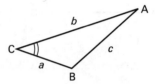

Area of this triangle is $\frac{1}{2} \times a \times b \times \sin C$
$= \frac{1}{2} ab \sin C$

Working with the cosine rule

If you have a problem involving 3 sides and 1 angle of a non-right-angled triangle then you can use the **cosine rule**.

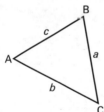

Use $a^2 = b^2 + c^2 - 2bc \cos A$

when you want to find a side.

Use $\cos A = \dfrac{b^2 + c^2 - a^2}{2bc}$

when you want to find an angle.

Practice Exercise

1

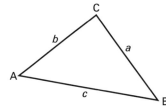

Say whether statements (a)–(d) are true or false.

(a) $a^2 = b^2 + c^2 - 2ab \cos C$

1 (a) Answer ....

(b) $\dfrac{\sin A}{a} = \dfrac{\sin B}{b}$

1 (b) Answer ....

(c) $\cos B = \dfrac{a^2 + c^2 - b^2}{2ac}$

1 (c) Answer ....

(d) $\dfrac{b}{\sin B} = \dfrac{c}{\sin C}$

1 (d) Answer ....

2

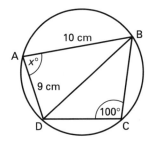

Find:

(a) angle $x°$ ....

(b) length BD ....

(c) area ABD. ....

3

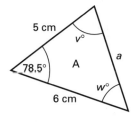
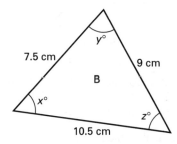

Use the sine and/or cosine rule to determine whether triangles A and B are similar.

....

....

....

Find the area of each triangle.

....

....

Shape, Space and Measures

Topic 14
Triangles and quadrilaterals

Examination Questions

1. These triangles are similar

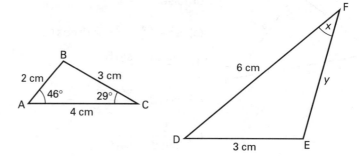

(a) What is the size of angle *x*?

.... degrees

(b) What is the length of *y*?

....

.... cm

(SEG – specimen paper)

2. The diagram shows part of the framework for a roof.

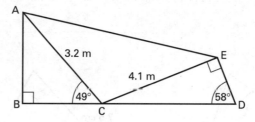

Triangles ABC and CED are right angled.
AC = 3.2 m   CE = 4.1 m
Angle ACB is 49°   Angle EDC is 58°

(a) Calculate the length BC.

....

....

....

(b) Calculate the length CD.

....

....

....

(NEAB, Winter 1998 – Paper 2)

Examination Questions

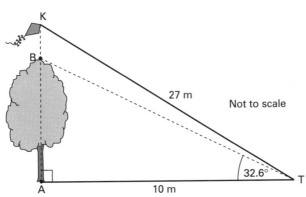

3. The diagram shows a kite, at K, flying directly above a tree.

From T, the angle of elevation to the top of the tree is 32.6° and AT = 10 m.

(a) Calculate AB, the height of the tree.

....

....

....

.... m

When the kite is directly above the tree, the length of the string, KT, is 27 m.

(b) Calculate the angle KTA.

....

....

....

.... degrees

(SEG, Winter 1998 – Paper 13)

Topic 14

Triangles and quadrilaterals

4. In the triangle XYL, AB is parallel to XY.
LA = 3 cm, LX = 8 cm and XY = 6 cm.
Find the length AB.

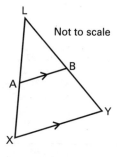

Not to scale

....

....

....

....

(NEAB – specimen paper)

5. In triangle ABC, AC = 4 cm, AB = 7 cm and angle ACB = 100°.
Calculate the area of the triangle.

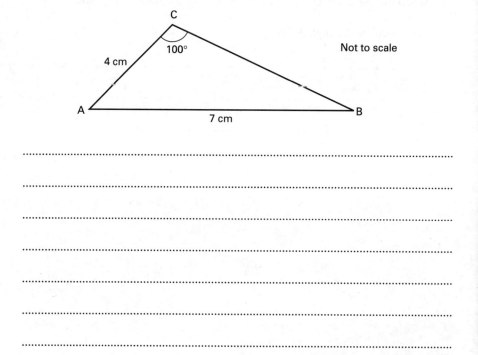

Not to scale

....

....

....

....

....

....

(SEG, Summer 1998 – Paper 15)

6.

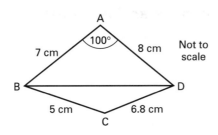

(a) Calculate the area of the triangle ABD.

....

....

....

....

(b) Calculate the length of BD.

....

....

....

....

(c) Calculate the size of the angle BCD.

....

....

....

....

(NEAB, Winter 1997 – Paper 1)

Topic 15

Measurement and drawings

Summary

Points of the compass and bearings

Make sure that you know the eight points of the compass and how these relate to bearings

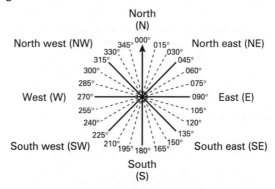

The direction of an object can be measured from a point using a (3 figure) bearing.

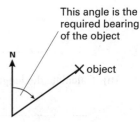

This angle is the required bearing of the object

Note: All bearings have 3 figures. You must write them all down even if the first figure is zero, i.e. 073°.

Like this

The bearing of a boat from a lighthouse is 073°. Find the bearing of the lighthouse from the boat.

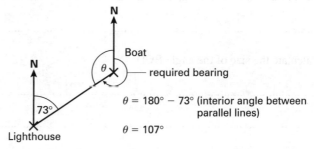

$\theta = 180° - 73°$ (interior angle between parallel lines)

$\theta = 107°$

The bearing of the lighthouse from the boat is $360° - 107° = 253°$

Basic units of measurement

Units of area

The area of a shape is measured by working out how many square units the shape covers.

The metric units of area are:

1 cm² = 1 cm × 1 cm = 10 mm × 10 mm = **100 mm²**
1 m² = 100 cm × 100 cm = **10 000 cm²**
1 km² = 1000 m × 1000 m = **1 000 000 m²**

Units of volume

The volume of a solid is measured by working out how many cubic units the shape contains.

The metric units of volume are:

1 cm³ = 1 cm × 1 cm × 1 cm = 10 mm × 10 mm × 10 mm = **1000 mm³**
1 m³ = 100 cm × 100 cm × 100 cm = **1 000 000 cm³**
1 km³ = 1000 m × 1000 m × 1000 m = **1 000 000 000 m³**

Practice Exercise

1 Add to the diagram:

   (a) a point B on a bearing of 060° from A

   (b) a point C on a bearing of 260° from A.

2

(a) Which point has co-ordinates $(-2, 3)$?

(b) Which point has co-ordinates $(1, -2)$?

(c) Which point has co-ordinates $(-2, -1)$?

(d) Which point has co-ordinates $(2, 1)$?

2 (a) Answer ....

2 (b) Answer ....

2 (c) Answer ....

2 (d) Answer ....

3 You travel 8 km in 1 hour.
Match the speeds with the units.

8	metres per minute
5	metres per second
$\dfrac{8 \times 1000}{60}$	miles per hour
$\dfrac{8 \times 1000}{60 \times 60}$	kilometres per hour

4 Complete the following:

   (a) $8\,cm^2 =$ .... mm^2

   (b) .... $km^2 = 5\,000\,000\,m^2$

   (c) $2.5\,m^2 =$ .... cm^2

   (d) $4\,m^3 =$ .... cm^3

   (e) .... $cm^3 = 100\,mm^3$

   (f) .... $km^3 = 2\,500\,000\,000\,m^3$

5 If the bearing of B from A is 060°, what is the bearing of A from B?

....

....

Summary

Locus of a point

The locus of a point is a fancy name to describe the path the point makes when it has to follow certain rules.

1   One fixed point
The locus of a point which is always the same distance, say 3 cm, from **one** given fixed point O, is a circle radius 3 cm centre O.

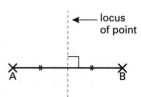

2   Two fixed points
The locus of a point which is always the same distance from **two** given fixed points, say A and B, is the perpendicular bisector of the line joining A to B.

3   One fixed line
The locus of a point which is always the same distance from **one** given fixed straight line is a pair of parallel lines joined by semicircles.

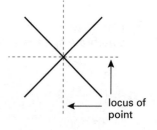

4   Two fixed lines
The locus of a point which is always the same distance from **two** given fixed intersecting lines is the bisectors of the angles between the lines.

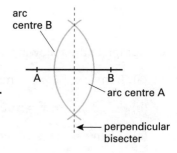

Constructions

You will need to know how to construct the following using ruler and compasses.

Perpendicular bisector of AB
With your compass point at A draw an arc.
With your compass point at B using the same radius draw another arc.
Join the points of intersection of these two arcs.
This is the perpendicular bisector of AB.

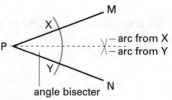

Angle bisector of ∠NPM
With your compass point at P draw an arc intersecting PM and PN at X and Y.
With your compass point at X draw an arc.
With your compass point at Y using the same radius draw another arc.
Join P and the point of intersection of these two arcs.
This is the bisector of the angle MPN.

Practice Exercise

1 Draw the locus of points:

(a) 2 cm from the line AB

(b) equidistant from points A and C.

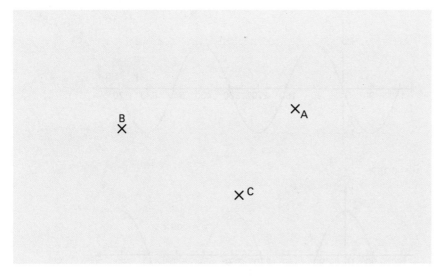

(c) Indicate the points which satisfy both of these conditions.

2 (a) Construct the perpendicular bisector of AD.

(b) Construct the bisector of angle BAC.

(c) Shade the region that is nearer to A than to D *and* nearer to AB than to AC.

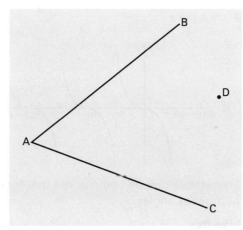

3 Construct the following on a separate sheet of paper using a ruler and compasses:

(a) an angle of 45°

(b) an angle of 60°

(c) an angle of 30°.

Summary

Sketching trig graphs

The graphs of $\sin x$ and $\cos x$ are a continuous wave form. The graph of $\tan x$ is discontinuous.

1 $y = \sin x$

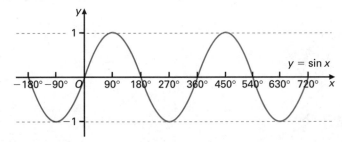

2 $y = \cos x$

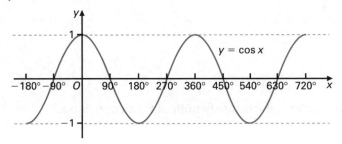

3 $y = \tan x$

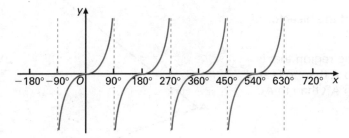

From these graphs you can see that trigonometric ratios can generate any number of angles.

Like this

Find the values of x between 0 and 360° for which $\sin x = 0.8$.

You must sketch the graph $y = \sin x$ and then draw the line $y = 0.8$.
Use your calculator to find the first x value which is 53.1°

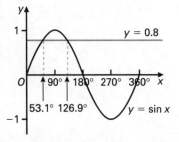

Use the symmetry properties of the sine graph to work out any other values.
The two values of x are 53.1° and $180° - 53.1° = 126.9°$

Practice Exercise

1 Use the graph to find all the values of x between 0° and 360° for which:

(a) $\sin x = 0.5$

(b) $\sin x = -0.3$

1 (a) Answer ....

1 (b) Answer ....

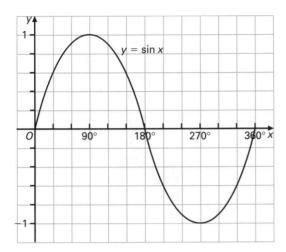

2 (a) On the same axes, sketch graphs of $y = \sin x$ and $y = \cos x$ for $0° \leqslant x \leqslant 360°$

(b) Use your graphs to estimate the values of x for which $\sin x = \cos x$

(c) Using your calculator or otherwise find the values for which $\sin x = \cos x$ as accurately as possible.

2 (b) Answer ....

....

2 (c) Answer ....

....

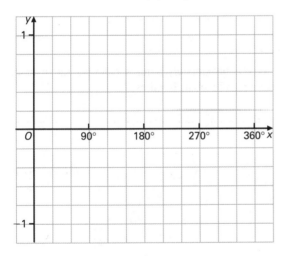

Topic 15

Measurement and drawings

Examination Questions

1. The diagram shows a map of Tasmania.

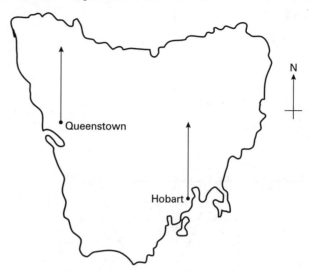

(a) What is the three figure bearing of Queenstown from Hobart?

....

The map has been drawn to a scale of 1 cm to 30 km

(b) (i) What is the actual distance between Queenstown and Hobart in kilometres?

....

....

(ii) By taking 8 km to be approximately 5 miles, calculate the distance between Queenstown and Hobart in miles.

....

....

(SEG – specimen paper)

Examination Questions

2. The diagram shows a map of a group of islands.
The map has been drawn to a scale of 1 cm to 5 km.

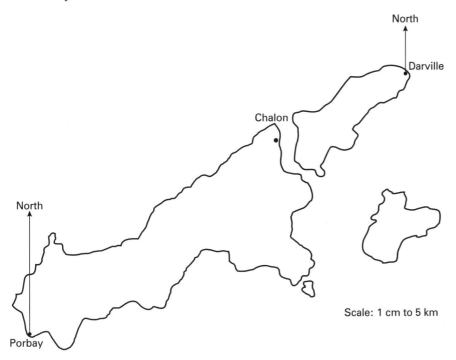

Scale: 1 cm to 5 km

(a) A straight road joins Porbay to Chalon.

    (i) Use the map to find the length of this road in kilometres.

    ....

    ....

    (ii) Brian cycles from Porbay to Chalon along this road.
        He sets off at 0930 and cycles at an average speed of 18 kilometres per hour.
        At what time does he arrive in Chalon?

    ....

    ....

    ....

(b) A lighthouse is on a bearing of 080° from Porbay and 200° from Darville.
Mark, with a cross, the position of the lighthouse on the map.

(SEG, Summer 1998 – Paper 14)

Examination Questions

Topic 15
Measurement
and drawings

3. The diagram shows a car par with ticket machines at P and Q.
People always use the ticket machine nearer to them.

Construct accurately and shade the region where people park who use machine P.

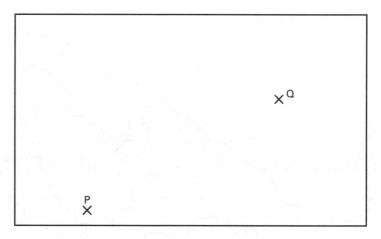

(NEAB, Winter 1997 – Paper 2)

4. The diagram shows the position of towns
Blackburn (B), Holywell (H) and Whitchurch (W).

Blackburn is 72 km north-east of Holywell.
Whitchurch is south-east of Holywell.
Blackburn is 86 km from Whitchurch.

(a) (i)   Calculate angle BWH

....

....

....

....

(ii) What is the three figure bearing of Blackburn from Whitchurch?

....

....

....

Examination Questions

(b) Castleford is 75 km due east of Blackburn.
Calculate the distance from Holywell to Castleford.

....

....

....

....

(NEAB – specimen paper)

5. Two straight roads are shown in the diagram.
A new gas pipe is to be laid from Bere equidistant from the two roads.

The diagram is drawn to a scale of 1 cm to 1 km.

(a) Construct, on the diagram, the path of the gas pipe.

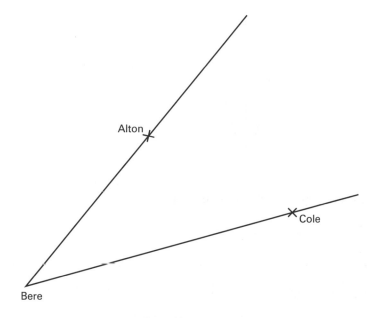

(b) The gas board needs a construction site depot.
The depot must be equidistant from Bere and Cole.
The depot must be less than 4 km from Alton.

(i) On the diagram draw loci to represent this information.

The depot must be nearer the road through Cole than the road through Alton.

(ii) Mark on the diagram with a cross a possible position for the site depot
which satisfies all of these conditions.

(SEG – specimen paper)

Topic 15

Measurement and drawings

Examination Questions

6. This is a sketch of the graph $y = \sin x$.

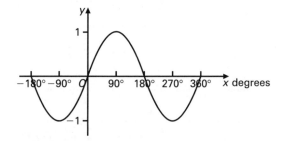

This is a sketch of a graph of the form $y = a \sin(x + b)$.

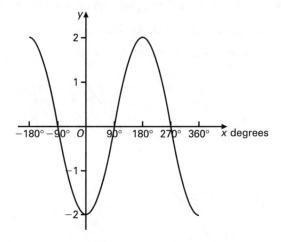

(a) Use the graphs find the values of a and b.

....

....

(b) Find all the solutions of the equation

$$3 \sin x = 2$$

between $x = 0$ and $x = 360°$

....

....

....

....

(NEAB – specimen paper)

7. The graph of $y = \sin x$ for $0° \leqslant x \leqslant 360°$ is drawn.

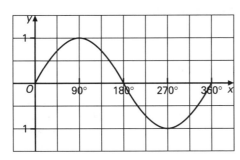

(a) (i) Angle p satisfies the equation $\sin p = \sin 210°$.
Angle p is not equal to $210°$.
What is the value of p?

....

(ii) Angle q satisfies the equation $\sin q = -\sin p$ where $0° \leqslant x \leqslant 360°$
Write down the possible values of q.

....

(b) On the same axes as $y = \sin x$, draw the graph of $y = \frac{1}{2}\cos x$ for $0° \leqslant x \leqslant 360°$.

(c) Use the graphs to solve the equation $\sin x = \frac{1}{2}\cos x$ for the range of x that the graph allows.

....

....

(NEAB – specimen paper)

Topic 16

Collection and representation

Summary

Displaying data

Data can be represented using some form of statistical diagram such as a pictogram, bar chart, line graph or pie chart.

Like this

The amount of money in £s taken in 'Clever Cloggs' school tuck shop is shown in the table:

Day	Monday	Tuesday	Wednesday	Thursday	Friday
Money	£1.40	£4.20	£12.30	£15.00	£7.10

Show the data using a line graph and a pie chart.

Line graphs

The information can be easily shown on a line graph although intermediate values on the graph may not have any meaning!

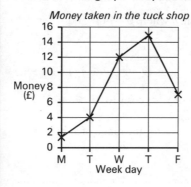

Pie charts

In a pie chart, the data is shared among 360° and the angle for each piece of data is worked out as follows:

Total money taken is £40.00   £40.00 is represented by 360°
                £1.00 is represented by 360° ÷ 40 = 9°

Angle for Monday is   1.40 × 9°   =   12.6°
Angle for Tuesday is   4.20 × 9°   =   37.8°
Angle for Wednesday is 12.30 × 9° = 110.7°
Angle for Thursday is   15.00 × 9° = 135°
Angle for Friday is   7.10 × 9°   =   63.9°
                        Total = 360°

Note: *It is a good idea to check that your angles do add up to 360° before proceeding.*

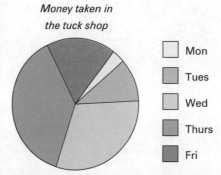

Money taken in the tuck shop

- Mon
- Tues
- Wed
- Thurs
- Fri

Practice Exercise

1 Complete the tally chart for the following data.

22	22	1	1	20	6	11	14	22	11	23	8	24
17	21	21	2	20	22	6	2	23	12	13	25	13
17	14	14	11	6	19	21	7	13	13	17	3	14
23	7	7	21	11	19	19	14	23	8	13	10	20
11	7	11	15	15	3	3	15	9	24	10	18	14
16	20	16	9	12	18	12	17	4	24	13	18	17

Number	Tally	Frequency
1–5		
6–10		
11–15		
16–20		
21–25		

2 (a) Complete the following to find the angles for the pie chart.

Favourite ice cream	vanilla	strawberry	chocolate	raspberry
Frequency	15	18	16	11

Total number of ice creams = ...

.... ice creams are represented by 360°

1 ice cream is represented by 360° ÷ .... = ...

Angle for vanilla is 15 × .... = ...

Angle for strawberry is 18 × .... = ...

Angle for chocolate is .... = ...

Angle for raspberry is .... = ...

(b) Use the information you have found in part (a) to complete the pie chart.

Favourite ice creams

Handling Data

Topic 16
Collection and representation

All about scatter diagrams

A scatter diagram is used to show whether or not there is a relationship between two variables. The distribution of points on the scatter diagram can be used to give an indication of the relationship or **correlation** between the two variables.

- If the points are randomly scattered you say there is **no correlation** between the two variables.

- If the points are close to a straight line you say there is **strong correlation**.

- If the points plotted are not close to a straight line you say there is **weak correlation**.

- If as one variable increases the other increases then you say there is **positive correlation**.

- If as one variable increases the other decreases then you say there is **negative correlation**

positive   negative
correlation   correlation

Line of best fit

Where the points plotted are close to a straight line then you can draw a line of best fit. The line of best fit should be drawn so that there are roughly as many points on one side of the line as the other.

Like this

The table gives the marks and time spent on a piece of homework undertaken by 6 pupils.

Pupil	A	B	C	D	E	F
Time (min)	60	55	30	10	40	55
Mark	9	8	6	1	6	7

Plot this data on a scatter diagram. Draw the line of best fit and comment on the correlation between the two sets of data.

It would seem that the more time spent on homework the better the mark.

There is fairly strong positive correlation between the two sets of data.

Note: You can use your line of best fit to estimate one of the variables if you are given the other.

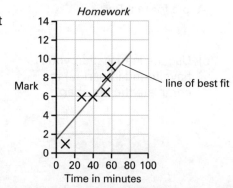

Homework

line of best fit

Practice Exercise

1 Link the scatter diagram to its description.
The first has been done for you.

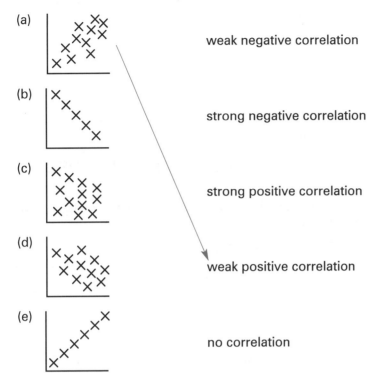

(a)

weak negative correlation

(b)

strong negative correlation

(c)

strong positive correlation

(d)

weak positive correlation

(e)

no correlation

2

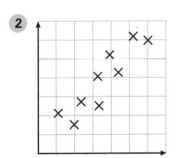

Draw a line of best fit on this scatter diagram.

3 Use the scatter diagram on page 160 of time spent on homework against time to answer the following:

(a) Calculate the likely time spent on a piece of homework by a pupil gaining a mark of 4.

3 (a) Answer ....

(b) Calculate the likely mark of a pupil spending 90 minutes on their homework.

3 (b) Answer ....

(c) Which of your answers to (a) and (b) is the more accurate? Why?

Topic 16

Collection and representation

Summary

Histograms

Histograms are similar to bar charts except that it is the area of each bar which represents the frequency.

The height of the bar is the **frequency density**.

and $$\text{frequency density} = \frac{\text{frequency}}{\text{class width}}$$

Like this

Draw a histogram of the data below showing the pocket money, £p, of pupils in a primary school.

Pocket money	$0 \leq p < 1.00$	$1.0 \leq p < 1.50$	$1.50 \leq p < 2.00$	$2.00 \leq p < 2.50$	$2.50 \leq p < 3.00$	$3.00 \leq p < 5.00$
Frequency	6	12	19	11	8	4

You should note that the classes are of unequal width, so you have to work out the frequency density.

First class width is 1 so frequency density is $6 \div 1 = 6$
Second class width is 0.5 so frequency density is $12 \div 0.5 = 24$ and so on.

Freq. density	$6 \div 1 = 6$	$12 \div 0.5 = 24$	$19 \div 0.5 = 38$	$11 \div 0.5 = 22$	$8 \div 0.5 = 16$	$4 \div 2 = 2$

Now mark the boundary of each class on the horizontal axis and plot the height as the frequency density on the vertical axis.

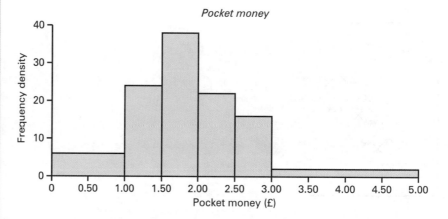

Note: If you are asked to work out the frequencies from a given histogram then use frequency = frequency density × class width.

Frequency polygon

A frequency polygon can be obtained from a bar chart or a histogram by joining up the mid points of the top of each bar with straight lines.

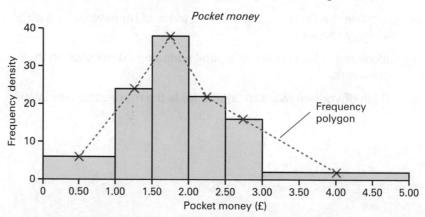

Practice Exercise

1 What is the difference between a histogram and a bar chart?

....

....

....

....

2 (a) Complete the following table showing the duration of telephone calls to work out the frequency densities.

Duration of call (to nearest minute	Frequency	Class width	Frequency density
1–3	18	3*	18 ÷ 3 = 6
4–6	24		
7–12	20		
13–24	17		

Note that the class width here is 3 minutes, as intervals will contain calls of durations from $\frac{1}{2}$ minute to $3\frac{1}{2}$ minutes.

(b) Show the information in the table as a histogram.

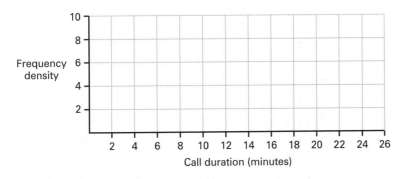

(c) Show the information in the table as a frequency polygon.

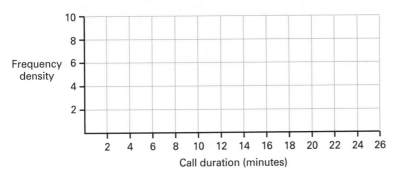

Examination Questions

1. In one week Ronnie rents out 90 items from his shop as shown in the table below.

Item	Frequency
Televisions	35
Videos	30
Computers	17
Other equipment	8

Complete the pie chart for all the week's rentals.

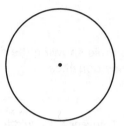

(NEAB, Summer 1998 – Paper 2)

2. The Mathematics scores and Science scores of 8 students are shown in the table.

Student	A	B	C	D	E	F	G	H
Mathematics score	44	18	51	60	25	10	35	40
Science score	34	21	46	50	18	15	29	39

(a) Use the data to plot a scatter diagram.

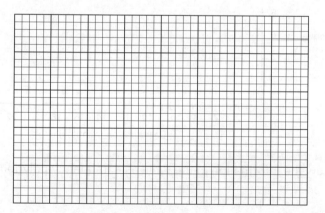

(b) What does the scatter diagram suggest about the connection between the scores in Mathematics and Science?

....

....

(SEG, Summer 1998 – Paper 12)

3. Each week during the summer season, a seaside resort recorded the rainfall in millimetres and the number of deck chair tickets sold.
The scatter diagram illustrates some of these recordings.

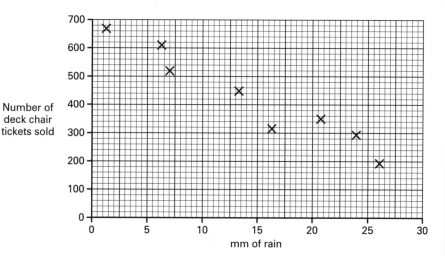

(a) What does the scatter diagram tell you about the connection between the rainfall and the number of deck chair tickets sold?

....

....

....

....

(b) On the diagram below, sketch what you might expect to get if you made a scatter diagram for 'the number of hours of sunshine' and 'the number of deck chair tickets sold' each week.

Number of
deck chair
tickets sold

Number of hours of sunshine

(NEAB – specimen paper)

Examination Questions

4. Some of the world records for running the mile are shown below. The data are represented on the scatter diagram.

Glenn Cunningham	1934	247 sec.
Roger Bannister	1954	239 sec.
Michael Jazy	1965	234 sec.
John Walker	1975	230 sec.
Steve Cram	1985	226 sec.

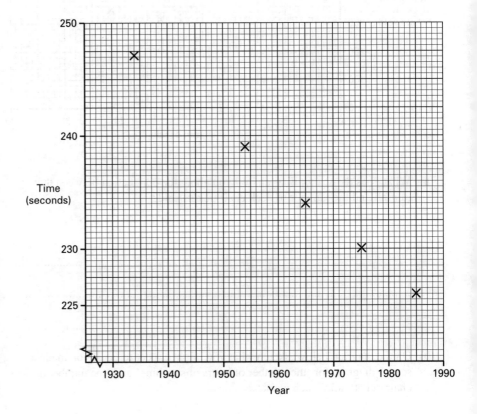

(a) Draw the line of best fit on the diagram.

(b) In 1979, Sebastian Coe ran a world record time.

Use your diagram to estimate this time.

....

....

(NEAB – specimen paper)

Examination Questions

5. A grouped frequency distribution table of the heights of 500 adult females is shown.

Height (*h* inches)	Frequency
$54.5 \leqslant h < 59.5$	1
$59.5 \leqslant h < 64.5$	115
$64.5 \leqslant h < 69.5$	380
$69.5 \leqslant h < 74.5$	4

(a) A frequency polygon showing the distribution of the heights of 500 adult males is shown. On the same axes, draw a frequency polygon for the heights of the females.

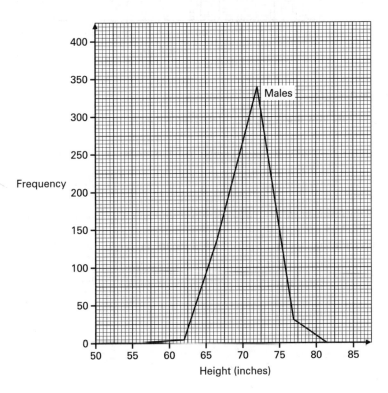

(b) Use the frequency polygons to compare these two distributions.

....

....

....

....

(SEG – specimen paper)

Topic 16

Collection and representation

6. The histogram shows the distribution of marks obtained by St Winifred's Year 11 pupils in their mock examinations.

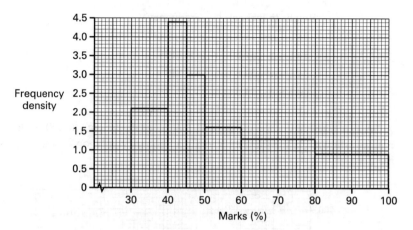

Use the histogram to

(a) estimate how many pupils gained between 50% and 60%

....

....

....

(b) find which mark range illustrated is the modal range.

....

....

....

(NEAB – specimen paper)

7. In a pilot survey some geography students were asked to use a local map to work out how far they lived from school.

The results are shown in this table.

Distance from school (km)	0–	0.5–	1–	2–	4–6
Frequency	11	14	15	12	8

(a) On the grid draw a histogram to illustrate this set of data.

....

....

....

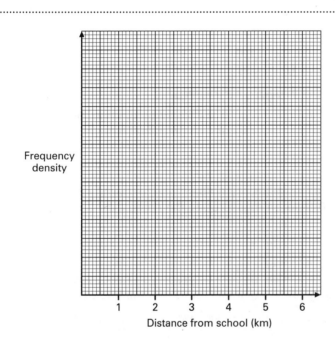

(b) In the actual survey the information was gathered from a 10% sample of the whole school population.

(i) Describe a suitable sampling method that could be used by the school

....

....

....

....

....

(ii) Give a reason for your choice.

....

....

(SEG, Summer 1998 – Paper 16)

Topic 17
Averages and spread

Finding the mean

To find the mean from a frequency table you use the formula: $\text{Mean} = \dfrac{\Sigma f \times x}{\Sigma f}$

where Σ is the greek letter sigma and stands for 'the sum of', x is the data value and f is the frequency.

Like this

The table gives the marks (x) scored in a Maths test. Find the mean mark.

Mark (x)	0	1	2	3	4	5
Frequency (f)	2	4	7	9	9	4

Sum of all the marks is
$\Sigma f \times x = (2 \times 0) + (4 \times 1) + (7 \times 2) + (9 \times 3) + (9 \times 4) + (4 \times 5) = 101$
Number tested is $\Sigma f = 2 + 4 + 7 + 9 + 9 + 4 = 35$

Mean mark is $\dfrac{\Sigma f \times x}{\Sigma f} = \dfrac{101}{35} = 2.89 \,(3\,\text{sf})$

Cumulative frequency graphs

Cumulative frequency graphs are found by plotting the cumulative frequencies at the upper values of the data. Then you join the points with a smooth curve.

Like this

Plot a cumulative frequency graph of the following data which shows the heights of 50 children measured to the nearest centimetre.

Height (cm)	$100 < h \le 110$	$110 < h \le 120$	$120 < h \le 130$	$130 < h \le 140$	$140 < h \le 150$	$150 < h \le 160$
Frequency	5	8	11	14	8	4

To plot the cumulative frequency graph you need to work out the cumulative frequencies by totalling (or accumulating) the frequencies in the table

Height (cm)	$100 < h \le 110$	$110 < h \le 120$	$120 < h \le 130$	$130 < h \le 140$	$140 < h \le 150$	$150 < h \le 160$
Frequency	5	8	11	14	8	4
Cumulative frequency	5	$5 + 8 = 13$	$13 + 11 = 24$	$24 + 14 = 38$	$38 + 8 = 46$	$46 + 4 = 50$

Note: Check that your final cumulative frequency is the same as the total.

Plot the cumulative frequency on the vertical axis and the upper value of the data (in this case height) on the horizontal axis and join the points with a smooth curve.

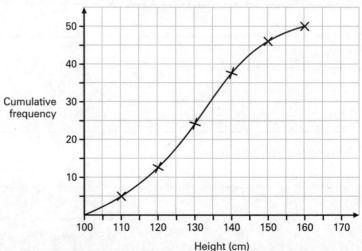

Practice Exercise

1 The table gives the marks (*x*) scored in an English test. Complete the table to find the mean mark.

Mark, x	Frequency, f	fx
0	0	$0 \times 0 = 0$
1	3	$1 \times 3 =$
2	11	
3	12	
4	5	
5	4	
	$\Sigma f =$	$\Sigma fx =$

$$\text{Mean} = \frac{\Sigma fx}{\Sigma f} = \frac{..........}{..........} = ...$$

Compare the mean of the English marks with the mean of the Maths marks on the opposite page. What do you notice?

....

....

2 The graph shows the cumulative frequency distribution of the Maths marks.

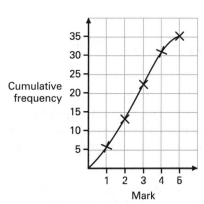

Complete the following table to work out the cumulative frequency of the English marks.

Plot the cumulative frequency distribution of the English marks on the same axes as the Maths marks.

Mark, x	Frequency, f	Cumulative frequency
0	0	0
1	3	3
2	11	
3	12	
4	5	
5	4	

Comment on your results.

....

....

Topic 17
Averages
and spread

Summary

Finding the mean of grouped data

To find the mean of grouped data you must work out the frequency times the mid-interval value of each group.

$$\text{Mean} = \frac{\Sigma(f \times \text{mid-interval value})}{\Sigma f}$$

Like this

Find the mean of the heights (h) of 80 children in a school from the data in the table below.

Height, h (cm)	$80 \leqslant h < 90$	$90 \leqslant h < 100$	$100 < h \leqslant 110$	$110 \leqslant h < 120$	$120 \leqslant h < 130$
Frequency	4	12	18	27	19

You must work out the mid-interval value of each group then the frequency times the mid-interval value.

Height, h (cm)	Frequency (f)	Mid-interval value (x)	$f \times$ mid-interval value ($f \times x$)
$80 \leqslant h < 90$	4	85	$4 \times 85 = 340$
$90 \leqslant h < 100$	12	95	$12 \times 95 = 1140$
$100 \leqslant h < 110$	18	105	$18 \times 105 = 1890$
$110 \leqslant h < 120$	27	115	$27 \times 115 = 3105$
$120 \leqslant h < 130$	19	125	$19 \times 125 = 2375$
	$\Sigma f = 80$		$\Sigma(f \times \text{mid-interval value}) = 8850$

Mean height is $\dfrac{\Sigma(f \times \text{mid-interval value})}{\Sigma f} = \dfrac{8850}{80} = 111$ (3 sf)

More cumulative frequency graphs

Cumulative frequency graphs are useful to show the spread of data and can be used to find the **median** (middle position), **quartiles** (first quarter and three-quarter positions) and **interquartile range** for a distribution.

Like this

For the data on page 170 which shows the heights of 50 children measured to the nearest centimetre find the median, quartiles and the interquartile range.

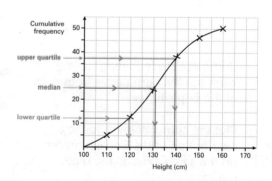

From your graph you can read off the following values:

The **median** is the 25th ($\frac{1}{2}$ of 50, the total frequency) value, approximately 131 cm.

The **lower quartile (LQ)** is the 12.5th ($\frac{1}{4}$ of 50) value, approximately 118 cm.

The **upper quartile (UQ)** is the 37.5th ($\frac{3}{4}$ of 50) value, approximately 139 cm.

The **interquartile range = upper quartile − lower quartile**
= 139 cm − 118 cm = 21 cm.

Practice Exercise

1 The table shows the heights of some seedlings grown in a greenhouse. Complete the table to find the mean height.

Height (cm)	Frequency, f	Mid-interval value, x	Frequency × mid-value
0 up to 2	8	1	$8 \times 1 = 8$
2 up to 6	12		
6 up to 10	13		
10 up to 20	8		
20 up to 40	5		
	$\Sigma f = $............		$\Sigma fx = $............

$$\text{Mean} = \frac{\Sigma fx}{\Sigma f} = \frac{............}{............} = ...$$

2 The following cumulative frequency curve gives the waiting time (in minutes) at a short-stay car park.

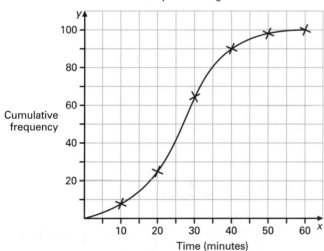

Car park waiting times

Use the graph to calculate:

(a) the median waiting time ....

(b) the upper quartile ....

(c) the lower quartile ....

(d) the interquartile range ....

Explain why the interquartile range is a good measure of range.

....

....

Topic 17
Averages and spread

Summary

Standard deviation

The standard deviation looks at the difference of each item of data from the mean of the data. Thus the standard deviation gives a measure of the spread of the data taking into account **every** bit of data.

There are two formulae for standard deviation, s.

1   Standard deviation, $s = \sqrt{\dfrac{\Sigma(x - \bar{x})^2}{n}}$ x is a given item of data,
$\bar{x}$ is the mean of the data,
n is the number of items of data,
and remember Σ means 'sum of.'

If you use that useful (and delightful) tool algebra (and a bit of statistics) the formula can be rearranged:

2   Standard deviation, $s = \sqrt{\dfrac{\Sigma x^2}{n} - \bar{x}^2}$

This formula is much easier to work with so do yourself a favour and learn it!

Like this

Find the standard deviation of these 5 test marks: 24, 46, 57, 68, 81.

You set out the results like this:

Mark x	x^2
24	576
46	2116
57	3249
68	4624
81	6561
Total marks $\Sigma x = 276$	$\Sigma x^2 = 17\,126$

Mean $\bar{x} = \dfrac{\text{total of marks}}{\text{number of marks}} = \dfrac{\Sigma x}{n} = \dfrac{276}{5} = 55.2$

Standard deviation, $s = \sqrt{\dfrac{\Sigma x^2}{n} - \bar{x}^2} = \sqrt{\dfrac{17\,126}{5} - 55.2^2} = 19.5 \,(3\,\text{sf})$

Note: For a grouped frequency distribution you use the mid-point values.

Standard deviation of a frequency distribution

To find the standard deviation for frequency and grouped frequency distributions use these formulae:

Standard deviation, $s = \sqrt{\dfrac{\Sigma f x^2}{\Sigma f} - \left(\dfrac{\Sigma f x}{\Sigma f}\right)^2}$

or $s = \sqrt{\dfrac{\Sigma f x^2}{\Sigma f} - \bar{x}^2}$ as $\bar{x} = \dfrac{\Sigma f x}{\Sigma f}$

Practice Exercise

1 Complete the table to calculate the mean and standard deviation for the following data.

Mark, x	Frequency, f	fx	fx^2
0	2	$2 \times 0 = 0$	$2 \times 0 \times 0 = 0$
1	4		
2	7		
3	9		
4	9		
5	4		
	$\Sigma f = \text{..........}$	$\Sigma fx = \text{..........}$	$\Sigma fx^2 = \text{..........}$

Mean, $\bar{x} = \dfrac{\Sigma fx}{\Sigma f} = \dfrac{\text{..........}}{\text{..........}} = \text{..........}$

Standard deviation, $s = \sqrt{\dfrac{\Sigma fx^2}{\Sigma f} - \left(\dfrac{\Sigma fx}{\Sigma f}\right)^2} = \sqrt{\dfrac{\text{..........}}{\text{..........}} - \left(\dfrac{\text{..........}}{\text{..........}}\right)^2}$

$= \text{..........}$

2 Complete the table to calculate the mean and standard deviation for the following data.

Height (cm)	Frequency, f	Mid-value, x	fx	fx^2
0 up to 2	8			
2 up to 6	12			
6 up to 10	13			
10 up to 20	8			
20 up to 40	5			
	$\Sigma f = \text{.........}$		$\Sigma fx = \text{.........}$	$\Sigma fx^2 = \text{.........}$

Mean, $\bar{x} = \dfrac{\Sigma fx}{\Sigma f} = \dfrac{\text{..........}}{\text{..........}} = \text{..........}$

Standard deviation, $s = \sqrt{\dfrac{\Sigma fx^2}{\Sigma f} - \left(\dfrac{\Sigma fx}{\Sigma f}\right)^2} = \sqrt{\dfrac{\text{..........}}{\text{..........}} - \left(\dfrac{\text{..........}}{\text{..........}}\right)^2}$

$= \text{..........}$

Handling Data

Topic 17
Averages
and spread

Examination Questions

1. (a) Pauline measures the length of some English cucumbers.
The lengths in centimetres are:

27, 28, 29, 30, 31, 31, 32, 33, 35, 37, 39

   (i) What is the range of the length of these cucumbers?

   ....

   (ii) What is the mean length of these cucumbers?

   ....

   ....

   Pauline measures the lengths of some Spanish cucumbers. The range of the lengths of these cucumbers is 6 cm and the mean is 30 cm.

   (b) Comment on the differences in these two varieties of cucumber.

   ....

   ....

   (SEG, Winter 1998 – Paper 14)

2. Year 11 pupils at Newtown School took part in a survey.
The results are shown in the table below.

Time to travel to school (t minutes)	Number of pupils
$0 < t \leqslant 5$	5
$5 < t \leqslant 10$	29
$10 < t \leqslant 20$	57
$20 < t \leqslant 30$	69
$30 < t \leqslant 45$	33
$45 < t \leqslant 75$	7
Over 75	0

Calculate the estimated mean travelling time of the pupils at Newtown School.

....

....

....

....

....

(NEAB – specimen paper)

Examination Questions

3. Fiaz records the number of words in each sentence of a magazine as shown in the following table.

Class interval	Frequency
1–5	13
6–10	24
11–15	22
16–20	15
21–25	13
26–30	8
31–35	3
36–40	1
41–45	0
46–50	1

(a) From the table:

(i) write down the modal class

    ....

(ii) write down the class interval in which the median lies

    ....

(b) Calculate an estimate of the mean number of words in each sentence.

    ....

    ....

    ....

    ....

    ....

    ....

Topic 17

Averages and spread

Examination Questions

4. The length of life of 100 batteries of a certain make were recorded. The table shows the results.

Length of life (hours)	<10	<15	<20	<25	<30	<35	<40
Cumulative frequency	0	2	9	50	86	96	100

(a) Draw a cumulative frequency graph to illustrate these data.

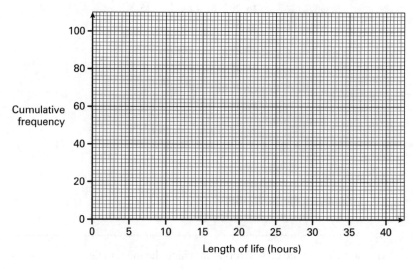

(b) How many batteries had a life of more than 32 hours?

....

(c) Use your graph to estimate:

    (i) the median;

    ....

    (ii) the interquartile range;

    ....

(d) Another make of battery has a median length of life of 25 hours and an interquartile range of 7 hours. Is this make of battery likely to be more reliable than the first?
Circle your answer yes/no.
Give a reason for your answer.

....

....

....

(SEG, Summer 1998 – Paper 14)

Examination Questions

5. The finishing times of 360 people who took part in a sponsored run are recorded. The following cumulative frequency graph shows these results.

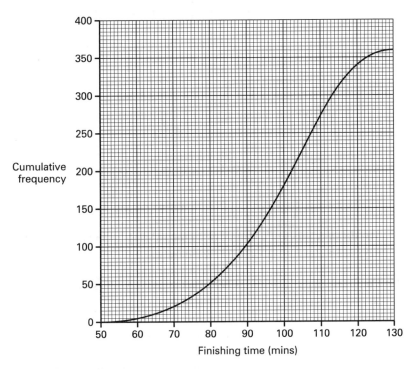

(a) What is the median finishing time?

....

(b) What is the interquartile range?

....

(SEG – specimen paper)

6. The delivery times in days of a sample of 20 first class letters are shown

```
1  1  3  1  1  1  1  1  2  1
1  2  4  1  1  1  1  1  2  1
```

(a) Calculate the mean and standard deviation of the delivery times

....

....

....

Mean............................... days

Standard deviation............................... days

The delivery times of a sample of 20 second class letters have a mean of 3.1 days and a standard deviation of 1.2 days.

(b) Comment on the differences between the delivery times for the first and second class letters.

....

....

....

During bad weather delivery times for second class letters are increased by one day.

(c) How does bad weather change the mean and the standard deviation of the delivery times for second class letters?

....

....

....

(SEG, Summer 1998 – Paper 15)

Examination Questions

7. In an experiment, Cathy has to take readings of radioactive emissions from six pieces of rock. Her readings are 490, 497, 511, 500, 479 and 484.

(a) Calculate the mean and standard deviation of her readings.

....

....

....

....

(b) Cathy's teacher then told her that the electronic counter she was using was faulty and each reading was 10 emissions too high.

Cathy used her original answers for the mean and standard deviation to write down their true values.

Explain how she did this.

....

....

....

....

(NEAB – specimen paper)

Topic 18
Probability

Summary

Total probability

The sum of all possible probabilities of an event is equal to 1 so that

P(event occurring) = 1 − P(event not occurring)

or **P(event not occurring) = I − P(event occurring)**

so that if the probability of doing my maths home work on time is 0.9 then the probability of not doing my maths homework on time is $1 - 0.9 = 0.1$

Expected probability

The expected number of times of getting a particular result is equal to the number of times multiplied by probability.

Like this

The probability of a rainy day in April is 0.4. How many rainy days would you expect to get in April?

There are 30 days in April, so expected number of rainy days is $30 \times 0.4 = 12$
You could expect 12 rainy days in April.

Showing probability

Probabilities of two events can be shown using a possibility space diagram.

Like this

Two dice are rolled. Show all the possible results in a table.

There are 36 possible results. In a table the results look like this.

		1	2	3	4	5	6
	1	1,1	2,1	3,1	4,1	5,1	6,1
	2	1,2	2,2	3,2	4,2	5,2	6,2
2nd dice	3	1,3	2,3	3,3	4,3	5,3	6,3
	4	1,4	2,4	3,4	4,4	5,4	6,4
	5	1,5	2,5	3,5	4,5	5,5	6,5
	6	1,6	2,6	3,6	4,6	5,6	6,6

1st dice

Possibility space diagram

Practice Exercise

1 The probability that a train arrives on time is 0.45.
The probability that a train arrives late is 20%.
What is the probability that it arrives early?
Explain how you reach your answer.

....

....

....

2 A square spinner is spun and a dice is rolled.

Complete the possibility space for the spinner and the dice.

			Spinner		
		Red (R)	Yellow (Y)	Green (G)	Blue (B)
Dice	1	1,R	1,Y	1,G	1,B
	2	2,R			
	3				
	4				
	5				
	6				

Use your possibility space to calculate:

(a) the probability of the spinner landing on yellow

(b) the probability of throwing a five with the dice

(c) the probability of throwing a three with the dice and the spinner landing on green

(d) the probability of the spinner landing on blue and throwing a six with the dice.

2 (a) Answer ....

2 (b) Answer ....

2 (c) Answer ....

2 (d) Answer ....

3 A dice is rolled and a coin is tossed. If a head is obtained then the score on the dice is doubled.
(a) Complete the following table.

				Dice			
		1	2	3	4	5	6
Coin	H	2					
	T	1					

(b) Use your table to calculate

(i) the probability of a score of 1

(ii) the probability of an even score

(iii) the probability of a score of 12.

(c) Which is the most likely score?

3 (b) (i) Answer ....

3 (b) (ii) Answer ....

3 (b) (iii) Answer ....

3 (c) Answer ....

Topic 18
Probability

Summary

More showing probability

Probabilities of more than one event can also be shown using a tree diagram.

Like this

A fair coin is tossed 3 times. Show all the possible results on a tree diagram.
$P(H)$ = probability of throwing a head, $P(T)$ = probability of throwing a tail

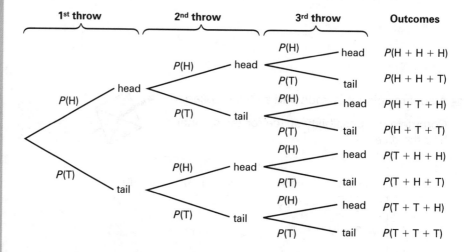

Mutually exclusive events

Mutually exclusive events can't happen at the same time, for example selecting an ace and a king when picking one card from a normal pack of playing cards.

If A and B can't happen at the same time then the probability of either one or the other happening is given by:

$$P(\textbf{A or B}) = P(\textbf{A}) + P(\textbf{B})$$

Like this

In a mixed bag of sweets the probability of picking a peppermint is 0.2 and the probability of picking a fruit drop is 0.3. What is the probability of picking a peppermint or fruit drop in any one go?

The events can't happen at the same time so they are mutually exclusive and the probability of picking a peppermint **or** a fruit drop is

$$P(\text{peppermint}) + P(\text{fruit drop}) = 0.2 + 0.3 = 0.5$$

Independent events

Independent events do not depend on each other, for example scoring an 'A' in Maths and winning your tennis match.

If A and B are independent events:

$$P(\textbf{A and B}) = P(\textbf{A}) \times P(\textbf{B})$$

Like this

A coin is tossed and a dice is rolled. What is the probability of obtaining a head and a six?

The results do not depend on each other so they are independent events and the probability of obtaining a head **and** a six $= P(\text{head}) \times P(\text{six}) = \dfrac{1}{2} \times \dfrac{1}{6} = \dfrac{1}{12}$

Practice Exercise

1. Say whether the events (a)–(d) are mutually exclusive or not.

   (a) Throwing a one and an even number on a dice.

   (b) Throwing a six and an even number on a dice.

   (c) Choosing a heart and a diamond from a pack of cards.

   (d) Choosing a king and a heart from a pack of cards.

1 (a) Answer ....

1 (b) Answer ....

1 (c) Answer ....

1 (d) Answer ....

2. Explain the difference between dependent and independent events.

   ....

   ....

   ....

   ....

3. A bag contains 4 red cubes and 5 blue cubes. A cube is taken from the bag and its colour noted. It is then returned to the bag. A second cube is then taken from the bag and its colour noted.

   (a) Complete the following tree diagram for choosing 2 cubes.

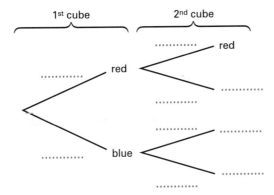

   (b) Use your tree diagram to calculate:

   (i) the probability of picking a red cube first followed by a blue cube.

   (ii) the probability of picking 2 blue cubes.

   (iii) the probability of picking a red cube and a blue cube in either order.

3 (b) (i) Answer ....

3 (b) (ii) Answer ....

3 (b) (iii) Answer ....

Topic 18
Probability

Dependent events

Dependent events do depend on each other and the outcome of the second event is conditional on the first event.

Like this

In a group of 500 pupils, 100 attend extra tuition. If a pupil has extra tuition the probability of them passing their exam is 0.87. If a pupil does not have extra tuition the probability of them passing their exam is 0.62. Draw a tree diagram showing the probabilities and use this to find the probability of a pupil having extra tuition and failing their exam.

You first work out the probabilities for the different branches like this:

Probability a pupil has extra tuition is $\dfrac{100}{500} = 0.2$

Probability a pupil does not have extra tuition is $1 - 0.2 = 0.8$

The probability of passing is **dependent** on having extra tuition so individual events are conditional upon one another as follows.

Note: The sum of the outcomes should also equal 1, so 0.174 + 0.026 + 0.496 + 0.304 = 1.

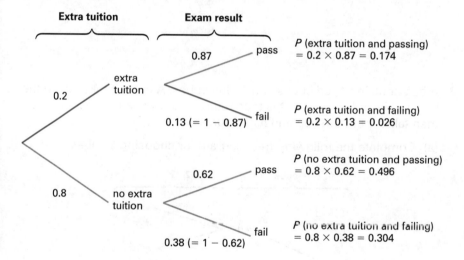

The branch in red gives the probability of having extra tuition and failing.

$P(\text{T and NP}) = 0.2 \times 0.13 = 0.026$

Practice Exercise

1 A bag contains 4 red cubes and 5 blue cubes. A cube is taken from the bag at random and its colour noted. The cube is **not** returned to the bag. A second cube is then taken from the bag and its colour noted.

(a) Complete the tree diagram for picking two cubes without replacement

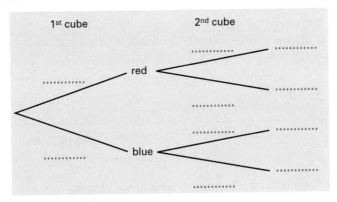

1st cube   2nd cube

red

blue

(b) Use your tree diagram to calculate:

  (i)   the probability of picking a red cube first followed by a blue cube

          1 (b) (i) Answer ....

  (ii)   the probability of picking 2 blue cubes

          1 (b) (ii) Answer ....

  (iii) the probability of picking a red cube and a blue cube in either order.

          1 (b) (iii) Answer ....

2 The diagram shows a series of road junctions.
At junction A the probability of a driver making a left turn is 0.3
At junction B the probability of a driver making a left turn is 0.1
At junction C the probability of a driver making a left turn is 0.4

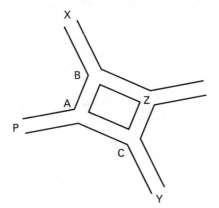

Calculate the probability that a driver starting from point P will arrive at:

(a) point X

          2 (a) Answer ....

(b) point Y

          2 (b) Answer ....

(c) point Z.

          2 (c) Answer ....

Topic 18
Probability

Examination Questions

1. Brenda has a bag of fruit sweets.
   There are 4 lemon, 1 orange, 8 strawberry and 7 pear sweets.
   Brenda chooses one sweet at random.

   What is the probability that it is:

   (a) the orange sweet?

   ....

   (b) a pear sweet?

   ....

   (c) not a pear sweet?

   ....

   (NEAB, Summer 1997 – Paper 2)

2. (a) A fair coin is thrown 20 times. It lands heads 12 times.
       What is the relative frequency of throwing a head?

       ....

       The coin continues to be thrown. The table shows the number of heads
       recorded for 20, 40, 60, 80 and 100 throws.

Number of throws	20	40	60	80	100
Number of heads	12	18	30	42	49

   (b) Draw a graph to show the relative frequency of throwing a head for these data.

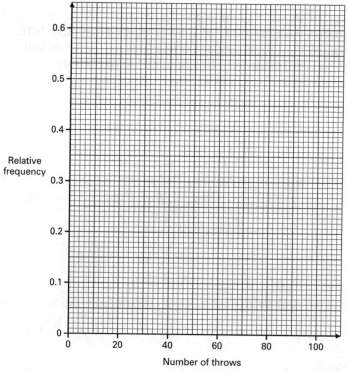

Relative frequency

Number of throws

   (c) Estimate the relative frequency of throwing a head for 1000 throws.

   ....

   (SEG, Winter 1998 – Paper 14)

3. Two fair spinners
are used for a game.
The scores from each
spinner are added together.

(a) Complete this table to show all possible totals for the two spinners.

	2	3	4	5	6
1	3	4			
2	4	5			
3					
4					
5					
6					

(b) What is the probability of scoring

(i) a total of 3?

....

(ii) a total of more than 8?

....

....

(NEAB, Summer 1998 – Paper 1)

4. When a model is fired in a kiln, the probability that it shrinks is 0.95.
When taken out to cool, the probability that it cracks is 0.04.

(a) What is the probability that when a model is fired it does **not** shrink?

....

(b) A model is fired in a kiln, then taken out to cool.
Complete the tree diagram by writing all the missing probabilities on the
appropriate branches

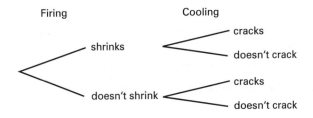

(c) Calculate the probability that the model shrinks and also cracks.

....

....

(NEAB, Summer 1997 – Paper 1)

Examination Questions

5. The table shows the colour and make of 20 cars.

		Colour of car	
		White	Blue
Make of car	Vauxhall	7	4
	Ford	3	6

(a) A car is chosen at random.
What is the probability that it is a blue Ford?

....

(b) A white car is chosen at random.
What is the probability that it is a Vauxhall?

....

(SEG, Winter 1998 – Paper 14)

6. The probability that I am late for work on a Monday is 0.4.
The probability that I am late for work on a Tuesday is 0.2.
What is the probability that in one particular week

(a) I am late for work on **both** Monday and Tuesday,

....

....

....

(b) I am late for work on Monday **but** on time on Tuesday,

....

....

....

(c) I am on time on **both** Monday and Tuesday,

....

....

....

(d) I am late for work on Monday **or** Tuesday but **not** both days?

....

....

....

....

(NEAB – specimen paper)

7. Whether or not Jonathan gets up in time for school depends on whether he remembers to set his alarm clock the evening before.
For 85% of the time he remembers to set the clock: the other 15% of the time he forgets.
If the clock is set, he gets up in time for school on 90% of the occasions.
If the clock is not set, he does not get up in time for school on 60% of the occasions.

On what proportion of the occasions does he get up in time for school?
(You may find a tree diagram will help you with your calculation.)

....

....

....

(NEAB, Winter 1997 – Paper 1)

8. A box of chocolates contains chocolates with three different centres as follows:
5 chocolates have toffee centres
7 chocolates have nougat centres
8 chocolates have caramel centres

Gary chooses two chocolates from the box

(a) What is the probability that they both have toffee centres?

....

....

(b) If the first chocolate that Gary chooses has a nougat centre

   (i) what is the probability that the next chocolate will have a caramel centre?

....

....

   (ii) what is the probability that the next chocolate will have a nougat centre?

....

....

Gary chooses three chocolates from the original selection

(c) What is the probability that each of them have a different centre?

....

....

....

Number

Topic 1: The rules of number

page 7

1 Any numbers a and b such that:
  a $47 < a < b < 48$
  b $23 < a < b < 2.4$
  c $0.25 < a < b < 0.267$
  d $0.037 < a < b < 0.043$

2 **Column 1   Column 2**

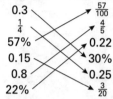

3

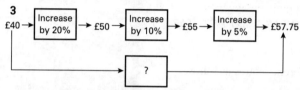

An increase of 20% followed by an increase of 10% followed by an increase of 5% is not the same as an increase of 35%.

page 9

1 Any fraction $\dfrac{a}{b}$ such that $\dfrac{2}{3} < \dfrac{a}{b} < \dfrac{3}{4}$

2 **a** and **d**

3 Cost is $117\frac{1}{2}\%$ (100% + $17\frac{1}{2}\%$ VAT)
  So $117\frac{1}{2}\%$ of the cost of the washing machine is £528.75
  1% of the cost of the washing machine is
  $\dfrac{£528.75}{117.5} = £4.50$
  100% of the cost of the washing machine is
  £4.50 × 100 = £450
  Cost of washing machine excluding VAT is £450

4 **b, d** and **e**

page 11

1    $1 \times 0.\dot{3}4\dot{5} = 0.345\,345\,345\ldots$
    $1000 \times 0.\dot{3}4\dot{5} = 345.345\,345\ldots$
    $999 \times 0.\dot{3}4\dot{5} = 345$
    $\therefore 0.\dot{3}4\dot{5} = \dfrac{345}{999} = \dfrac{115}{333}$

2 Rational: $\sqrt{4}$, $\sqrt[3]{8}$
  Irrational: π, $\sqrt{2}$, $\sqrt{3}$, $\sqrt{2}+1$, π^2, $\sqrt[3]{2}$

3 a $\sqrt{20} + \sqrt{12} = \sqrt{4 \times 5} + \sqrt{4 \times 3} = \sqrt{4} \times \sqrt{5} + \sqrt{4} \times \sqrt{3}$
      $= 2\sqrt{5} + 2\sqrt{3} = 2(\sqrt{5} + \sqrt{3})$
  b $\sqrt{63} - \sqrt{28} = \sqrt{9 \times 7} - \sqrt{4 \times 7} = 3\sqrt{7} - 2\sqrt{7} = \sqrt{7}$
  c $\dfrac{\sqrt{50}}{\sqrt{2}} = \dfrac{\sqrt{25 \times 2}}{\sqrt{2}} = \dfrac{5\sqrt{2}}{\sqrt{2}} = 5$
  d $\dfrac{\sqrt{27}}{\sqrt{3}} = \dfrac{\sqrt{9 \times 3}}{\sqrt{3}} = \dfrac{3\sqrt{3}}{\sqrt{3}} = 3$

4 a $\dfrac{15\sqrt{2}}{\sqrt{5}} = \dfrac{15\sqrt{2} \times \sqrt{5}}{\sqrt{5} \times \sqrt{5}} = \dfrac{15\sqrt{2 \times 5}}{5} = 3\sqrt{10}$
  b $\dfrac{50}{\sqrt{2}} = \dfrac{50 \times \sqrt{2}}{\sqrt{2} \times \sqrt{2}} = \dfrac{50\sqrt{2}}{2} = 25\sqrt{2}$
  c $\dfrac{75}{\sqrt{10}} = \dfrac{75 \times \sqrt{10}}{\sqrt{10} \times \sqrt{10}} = \dfrac{75\sqrt{10}}{10}$

Topic 2: More number

page 17

1 *Example:* $-6 + 1 + -3 + 7 + -1 + 2 = 0$

2 To make 100 ml of salad dressing, you need 80 ml oil and 20 ml vinegar.

3 The ratio of males to females is 7 : 3

4 2.48

5 a ✓   b ✗   c ✗   d ✗   e ✓

page 19

1 3040 (3 sf); 3039.7 (1 dp); 3040 (nearest whole number); 3000 (1 sf)

2 3 and 3039

3 0.0063, $6.3 \div 10^2$, 0.63×10^3, 63×100, 6.3×10^4

4 $0.9 \div -0.3 =$ -30
   $-3 \times -9 =$ $+30$
   $-9 \div 0.3 =$ -3
   $-3 \div 9 =$ $-\frac{1}{3}$
   $-9 \div -0.3 =$ $+27$

page 21

1 a

  correct to the nearest metre ——→ $2.95 \leqslant x < 3.05$
  correct to the nearest cm ——→ $2.5 \leqslant x < 3.5$
  correct to the nearest 10 cm ——→ $2.995 \leqslant x < 3.005$

  b Upper bound = 3.025 m; lower bound = 2.975 m

2 Upper bounds of suitcase weight; 19.5 kg, 21.5 kg, 13.5 kg, 17.5 kg
  Upper bound of total weight = 19.5 + 21.5 + 13.5 + 17.5 = 72 kg
  So it would not be safe to put them on a trolley that can take a maximum weight of 70 kg

Topic 3: Describing number

page 27

1 4.5×10^7

2 $240 = 2 \times 120$
      $= 2 \times 2 \times 60$
      $= 2 \times 2 \times 2 \times 30$
      $= 2 \times 2 \times 2 \times 2 \times 15$
      $= 2 \times 2 \times 2 \times 2 \times 3 \times 5$
      $= 2^4 \times 3 \times 5$

3 $2 = \sqrt{4}$; $3 = \sqrt{9}$; $4^2 = 16$; $9^2 = 81$

4 a 432 000   b 206   c 0.008 15

page 29

1 ab^2, bab, b^2a
  a^2b^2, $ab \times ab$, $(ab)^2$, $\sqrt{a^4b^4}$, $\dfrac{a^3b^3}{ab}$
  a^2b, ba^2, $a \times a \times b$
  ab, $\dfrac{a^2}{a} \times \dfrac{b^2}{b}$, $\sqrt{a^2b^2}$, $\dfrac{(ab)^2}{ab}$

2 0.000 48, 2.4×10^{-3}, 4.8×10^{-3}, 0.48, 2.4, 240, 4.8×10^2, 2.4×10^3

3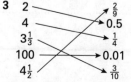

  2            $\frac{2}{9}$
  4   0.5
  $3\frac{1}{3}$ $\frac{1}{4}$
  100   0.01
  $4\frac{1}{2}$ $\frac{3}{10}$

4 a The highest common factor (HCF) of two numbers is the largest integer which is a factor of both numbers.

b The lowest common multiple (LCM) of two numbers is the lowest number for which both numbers are factors.

page 31

1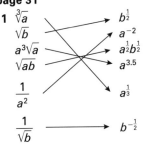

$\sqrt[3]{a}$ $\quad$ $b^{\frac{1}{2}}$

$\sqrt{b}$ $\quad$ a^{-2}

$a^3\sqrt{a}$ $\quad$ $a^{\frac{1}{2}}b^{\frac{1}{2}}$

$\sqrt{ab}$ $\quad$ $a^{3.5}$

$\dfrac{1}{a^2}$ $\quad$ $a^{\frac{1}{3}}$

$\dfrac{1}{\sqrt{b}}$ $\quad$ $b^{-\frac{1}{2}}$

2 a $64^{\frac{3}{2}} = (\sqrt{64})^3 = 8^3 = 512$

b $(\frac{1}{2})^{-2} = 2^2 = 4$

c $(\frac{1}{4})^{-\frac{1}{2}} = 4^{\frac{1}{2}} = \sqrt{4} = 2$

d $\sqrt[4]{81} = 3$

Topic 4: Application of number

page 37

1 Small size: 1 m/ costs £1.29 ÷ 100 = £0.0129
Large size: 1 m/ costs £3.10 ÷ 250 = £0.0124
Best buy is the large size
Check
Small size: 1 penny buys 100 ÷ 129 = 0.775 m/
Large size: 1 penny buys 250 ÷ 310 = 0.806 m/
Best buy is large size

2 Discount = $\dfrac{5}{100} \times$ £57.45 = £2.87 (to nearest penny)

Price paid – £57.45 – £2.87 = £54.58

3 b gives the correct answer

page 39

1 Tax paid at 20% = 0.2 × £3900 = £780
Tax paid at 23% = 0.23 × (£16 500 − £3900) = £2898
Total tax paid = £780 + £2898 = £3678

2 First find the volume of cuboid in cm³.
To find the mass (in g) you multiply the volume (in cm³) by the density (in g/cm³).

3 Interest for 1st year = $\dfrac{3}{100} \times$ £100 = £3

Amount at beginning of 2nd year = £100 + £3 = £103

Interest for 2nd year = $\dfrac{3}{100} \times$ £103 = £3.09

∴ Amount at end of 2nd year = £103 + £3.09 = £106.09

4 a £100 × (1.03)² = £106.09

b Answers are the same. Multipliers for percentage increase can be used to calculate compound interest.

page 41

1 a Neither
b Inversely proportional
c Directly proportional
d Inversely proportional
e Directly proportional
f Directly proportional

2 y varies inversely as x: $y \propto \dfrac{1}{x}$

y is proportional to x: $y \propto x$

y is inversely proportional to the square root of x:

$\qquad y \propto \dfrac{1}{\sqrt{x}}$

y is proportional to the cube root of x: $y \propto x^{\frac{1}{3}}$

y varies as the cube of x: $y \propto x^3$

y is inversely proportional to x cubed: $y \propto x^{-3}$

3 $P = k\sqrt{Q}$, so $k = \dfrac{\sqrt{Q}}{P} = \dfrac{\sqrt{100}}{6} = \dfrac{10}{6}$ So $P = \dfrac{10}{6}\sqrt{Q}$

When $Q = 64$, $P = \dfrac{10}{6} \times \sqrt{64} = \dfrac{80}{6} = 13\frac{1}{3}$

Algebra

Topic 5: The language of algebra

page 47

1 Like terms: $x, 3x, 5x, -2x$; $2y, 7y, -\frac{1}{2}y, \frac{1}{3}y$; $z, 4z$; $xy, 3xy - yx$; $xyz, 2xyz, \frac{1}{2}zyx$

2 a $6y$ $\qquad$ **c** a^2b^2 (or $abab$) $\qquad$ **e** $4x + 8$
  b $2ab$ $\qquad$ **d** $3x$ (or $ba + ab$) $\qquad$ **f** $y^2 - 3y$

3 $3(x - 6)$ $\quad$ $18 - 3x$ $\quad$ $-3(-6 + x)$
  $3(6 - x)$ $\quad$ $3x + 18$ $\quad$ $-3(x + 6)$
  $3(x + 6)$ $\quad$ $-3x - 18$ $\quad$ $-3(-x - 6)$
  $3(-x - 6)$ $\quad$ $3x - 18$ $\quad$ $-3(-x + 6)$

4 Let the number be x, the answer y.

Then $y = \left(\dfrac{2x + 6}{2}\right) - x = x + 3 - x = 3$

5 ab^2

page 49

1 Area of A $= x^2$; Area of B $= 8x$; Area of C $= 5x$;
Area of D $= 5 \times 8 = 40$
Total area $= x^2 + 8x + 5x + 40$
$\qquad\qquad = x^2 + 13x + 40$

2 $(x + 12)^2 = (x + 12)(x + 12) = x^2 + 12x + 12x + 144$
$\qquad\qquad\qquad\qquad = x^2 + 24x + 144$

3 a $(x + 7)(x + 2) = x^2 + 7x + 2x + 14 = x^2 + 9x + 14$
  b $(x - 3)(x + 8) = x^2 - 3x + 8x - 24 = x^2 + 5x - 24$
  c $(x - 5)(x - 11) = x^2 - 5x - 11x + 55 = x^2 - 16x + 55$

4 a $x^2 + 5x + 4 = (x + 1)(x + 4)$
  b $x^2 + 6x - 7 = (x + 7)(x - 1)$
  c $x^2 - x - 6 = (x - 3)(x + 2)$
  d $x^2 - 11x + 24 = (x - 3)(x - 8)$

page 51

1 a $4x^2 - 25 = (2x)^2 - 5^2 = (2x + 5)(2x - 5)$
  b $25a^2 - 16b^2 = (5a)^2 - (4b)^2 = (5a + 4b)(5a - 4b)$

2 a C $\qquad\qquad$ **b** B

3 a $(2x - 11)(x - 2)$
  b $(4x - 1)(x + 3)$
  c $(2x + 5)(3x - 2)$

4 Incorrect: $10p^3q^3, 10pq^3, 10q^3p^3, 16p^2q^2$
Correct but not fully simplified: $16pq^2p^2q, 16p^2qpq^2$
Correct and fully simplified: $16(pq)^3, 16p^3q^3$

Topic 6: Making graphs

page 57

1 a $(-4, 4), (-2, 2), (0, 0), (2, -2)$
  b $(-8, 0), (-6, 1), (-4, 2), (-2, 3)$
  c $(-4, 7), (-2, 1), (0, -5), (2, -11)$
  d $(4, -4); (0, 4), (4, -17)$

2

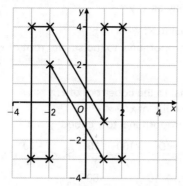

3 a

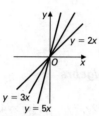

$y = 2x$
$y = 3x$
$y = 5x$

c

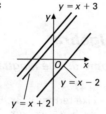

$y = x + 3$
$y = x - 2$
$y = x + 2$

b

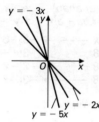

$y = -3x$
$y = -2x$
$y = -5x$

d

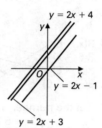

$y = 2x + 4$
$y = 2x - 1$
$y = 2x + 3$

page 59

1 a

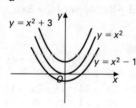

$y = x^2 + 3$
$y = x^2$
$y = x^2 - 1$

c

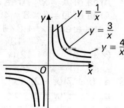

$y = \frac{1}{x}$
$y = \frac{3}{x}$
$y = \frac{4}{x}$

b

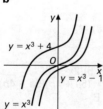

$y = x^3 + 4$
$y = x^3$
$y = x^3 - 1$

d

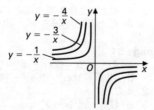

$y = -\frac{4}{x}$
$y = -\frac{3}{x}$
$y = -\frac{1}{x}$

2 a $\dfrac{2}{x}$ (B)   **b** x^3 (C)   **c** $(x-2)(x-3)$ (A)

page 61

1 a

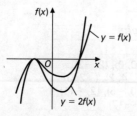

$y = f(x)$
$y = 2f(x)$

b

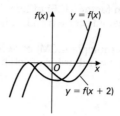

$f(x)$ $y = f(x)$
$y = f(x + 2)$

c

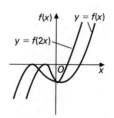

$f(x)$ $y = f(x)$
$y = f(2x)$

2 a

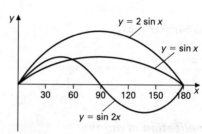

$y = 2 \sin x$
$y = \sin x$
$y = \sin 2x$

b

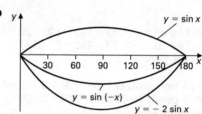

$y = \sin x$
$y = \sin (-x)$
$y = -2 \sin x$

c

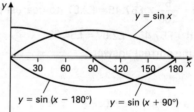

$y = \sin x$
$y = \sin (x - 180°)$ $y = \sin (x + 90°)$

Topic 7: Using graphs

page 65

1 C

2 a 12:45   **b** 45 minutes

3

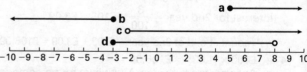

4 a $x \geqslant 3$ **c** $x > -3$
  b $x \leqslant -1$ **d** $-5 < x \leqslant 2$

page 67

1 *Smallest gradient* $3y = x - 1$

$y = \dfrac{x}{2} + 10$

$5y = 8x$

Largest gradient $y = 2x + 3$

2 a D   **b** A   **c** B   **d** C

3

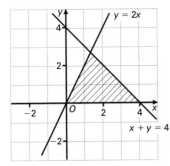

4 a $m = 3, c = 2$ **d** $m = \frac{1}{2}, c = 1$
  b $m = -2, c = 7$ **e** $m = -2, c = 3$
  c $m = 2, c = -\frac{1}{2}$

page 69
1 **a** False   **c** True   **e** True
  b False   **d** False
2 **a** C
  b p is the gradient, q is the intercept on the y axis
3 $x = -3, x = 2$

Topic 8: Using algebra

page 77
1 **a** 1 kg **b** 5 kg **c** 2 kg **d** 5 kg **e** 5 kg **f** 3 kg
2 A and C
3 $3x + 75 = 360$
  $3x = 285$
  $x = 95$
4 $a + c = 3\frac{1}{2}; bc = 1; ad = -1; ad + bc = 0;$
  $a(b + d) = 5; a^b = 9; b^a = 8; a(b - d) = 7$

page 79
1 **a** Either $(x - 3) = 0$ or $(x + 7) = 0$
    $x = 3$ or $x = -7$
  b Either $(x + 7) = 0$ or $(2x - 5) = 0$
    $x = -7$ or $x = \frac{5}{2}$
  c $(x + 5)(x - 3) = 0$
    Either $(x + 5) = 0$ or $(x - 3) = 0$
    $x = -5$ or $x = 3$
  d $(x - 7)(x + 4) = 0$
    Either $(x - 7) = 0$ or $(x + 4) = 0$
    $x = 7$ or $x = -4$
2 $x^2 - 7x - 12 = 0; x = 4, x = 3$
  $x^2 + x - 12 = 0; x = -4, x = 3$
  $x^2 - x - 12 = 0; x = 4, x = -3$
  $x^2 + 7x + 12 = (x + 4)(x + 3); x = -4, x = -3$
3 **a** $x = 3, y = 5$ **b** $x = 2, y = -3$

page 81
1 $x = \frac{1}{3}$ or $x = -2$
2 $x = 0.477$ (3 sf) or $x = -1.68$ (3 sf)

Topic 9: More using algebra

page 85
1 $4n$; 4, 8, 12, 16, ... $3n + 2$; 5, 8, 11, 14
  $n + 3$; 4, 5, 6, 7, ... $6n$; 6, 12, 18, 24, ...
  $n + 4$; 5, 6, 7, 8, ...
2 nth term $= -3n + 21$
3 **a** $5 > 3$ **c** $3^2 > 6$
  b $-2 < 4$ **d** $0.25 > 0.2$
4 $y - c = mx$
  $\dfrac{y - c}{m} = x$
  $x = \dfrac{y - c}{m}$

page 87
1 A
2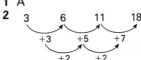

nth term $= 3 + 3(n - 1) + 1(n - 1)(n - 2)$
  $= 3 + 3n - 3 + n^2 - 3n + 2 = n^2 + 2$
3 Sequence: 4, 12, 24, 40, ...
  1st differences: 8, 12, 16, ...
  2nd differences: 4, 4
  nth term $= 4 + 8(n - 1) + 2(n - 1)(n - 2)$
    $= 4 + 8n - 8 + 2n^2 - 6n + 4$
    $= 2n^2 + 2n$
4 **a** $x > 4$ **b** $x \leqslant 6$ **c** $x > \frac{5}{2}$
5 A

page 89
1 $y = \dfrac{x - 2}{x - 1}$
  $y(x - 1) = x - 2$
  $xy - y = x - 2$
  $xy - x = y - 2$
  $x(y - 1) = y - 2$
  $x = \dfrac{y - 2}{y - 1}$

2 **a**
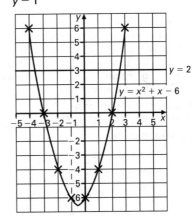

The solution to the inequality $x^2 + x - 6 \leqslant 0$ is the portion of the curve which lies below the x axis, i.e. $-3 \leqslant x \leqslant 2$
  b $x^2 + x - 6 \leqslant 2$ (draw the line $y = 2$)
    $-3.25 \leqslant x \leqslant 2.25$

3
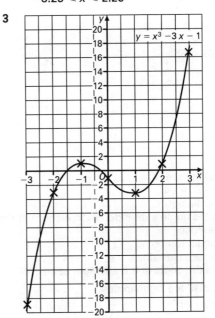

$$x^3 - 3x - 1 = 0$$
$$x = -1.5, -0.5, 1.8$$

Value of x	Value of y	
-1.5	0.125	too big
-1.6	-0.296	too small
-1.55	-0.074	too small
-1.53	-0.024	too small
-1.52	0.048	too big
-1.525	0.028	too big

Solution lies between -1.525 and -1.53
Therefore $x = -1.53$ (2 dp)

Shape, Space and Measures

Topic 10: Angle properties

page 95
1 a $f = 135°$, $g = 45°$, $h = 135°$ **d** $q = 57°$
   b $i = 90°$ **e** $r = 73°$, $s = 92°$
   c $j = 80°$, $k = 100°$, $l = 80°$, $m = 80°$, $n = 100°$, $o = 80°$, $p = 100°$
2 a $a = 108°$; angles on a straight line
      $c = d$; alternate angles
      $b = 72°$; vertically opposite angles
      $e = 72°$; corresponding angles
3 a False **c** True **e** True
   b False **d** False **f** False
4 a If DA and CB were parallel, then
      $\hat{ADC} + \hat{DCB} = 180$. In this case
      $\hat{ADC} + \hat{DCB} = 65° + 121° = 186°$, therefore DA
      and CB are not parallel.
   b $\hat{ABC} = 59°$; interior angles
      $\hat{DAB} = 115°$; interior angles

page 97
1 a $900°$
   b $1440°$
2 a $(n - 2) \times 180° = (6 - 2) \times 180° = 720°$
   b Hexagon consists of 4 triangles, so angle sum $= 4 \times 180° = 720°$

   c $120°$ ($720° \div 6$)
3 a False **d** False
   b False **e** True
   c True

page 99
1 a $a = b = 40°$
   b $c = 74°$
   c $d = 45°$
2 a Cyclic quadrilateral
   b $a = 180 - 86 = 94°$
3 Line AB is a diameter
4 a …twice the angle subtended by the chord at the circumference.
   b …add up to $180°$.
   c …are equal in length.
   d …equals the angle in the alternate segment.
5 $\hat{CFD}$, $\hat{ADC}$, $\hat{BDC}$ are right angles
   $\hat{ADF} = \hat{DEF} = \hat{DCF}$

Topic 11: Length, area and volume

page 105
1 C and D
2 Area of A $= 6 \times 10 = 60\,\text{cm}^2$
   Area of B $= 6 \times 7 = 42\,\text{cm}^2$
   Total area $= 60 + 42 = 102\,\text{cm}^2$
3 a $51\,\text{cm}^2$ **b** $152\,\text{cm}^2$

page 107
1 Area of parallelogram = base $\times$ height
   Area of trapezium = half height $\times$ sum of parallel sides
   Volume of cylinder = area of base $\times$ height
2 Smallest area C, E, B, F, D, A Largest area
3 a $\frac{1}{2}(3 \times 4) \times 10 = 60\,\text{cm}^2$
   b $6 \times 3 \times 10 = 180\,\text{cm}^2$
   c $\frac{4}{2}(8 + 11) \times 10 = 380\,\text{cm}^2$
   d $\pi \times 6^2 \times 10 \times 1130\,\text{cm}^2$ (3 sf)
4 Lengths: $a + b + c$, $2a + 2b$, $4(a + b + c)$
   Areas: πa^2, $ab + ac$, $a^2 + b^2$
   Volumes: abc, a^2b

page 109
1 a Surface area (with base) $= (\pi \times 3^2) + (\pi \times 3 \times 5) = 24\pi$
      $= 75.4\,\text{cm}^2$ (3 sf)
      Volume $= \frac{1}{3}(\pi \times 3^2 \times 4) = 12\pi = 37.7\,\text{cm}^3$ (3 sf)
   b Surface area (with base) $= \frac{1}{2} \times 4 \times \pi \times 5^2 + \pi \times 5^2$
      $= 75\pi = 235.6\,cm^2$ (1 dp)
      Volume $= \frac{2}{3} \times \pi \times 5^3 = \frac{250}{3}\pi = 261.8\,\text{cm}^3$ (1 dp)
2 a Arc length $= \frac{1}{4} \times 10\pi = 2.5\pi = 7.85\,\text{cm}$ (3 sf)
      Sector area $= \frac{1}{4} \times 25\pi = \frac{25}{4}\pi = 19.6\,\text{cm}^2$ (3 sf)
   b Arc length $= \frac{1}{18} \times 8\pi = \frac{4}{9}\pi = 1.40\,\text{cm}$ (3 sf)
      Sector area $= \frac{1}{18} \times 16\pi = \frac{8}{9}\pi = 2.79\,\text{cm}^2$ (3 sf)
   c Arc length $= \frac{17}{18} \times 8\pi = \frac{68}{9}\pi = 23.7\,\text{cm}$ (3 sf)
      Sector area $= \frac{17}{18} \times 16\pi = \frac{136}{9}\pi = 47.5\,\text{cm}^2$ (3 sf)
3 a $\frac{\pi}{4}(7^2 - 6^2) = \frac{13}{4}\pi$
   b $\frac{5}{18}\pi(6^2 - 4^2) = \frac{50}{9}\pi$

Topic 12: Symmetry and transformations

page 117
1 a 3 **c** infinite number
   b 6 **d** 5
2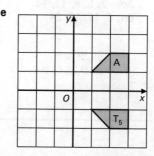
3 a T_2 **b** T_3 **c** T_1 **d** T_4
   e

4

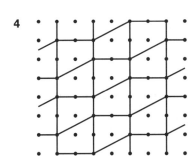

1 a, b

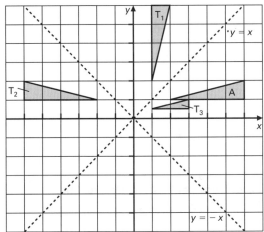

c Reflection in the line $x = 0$
d T_3 is an enlargement of A with scale factor $\frac{1}{2}$ centre (0, 0).
e The co-ordinates of A after a translation with vector $\begin{pmatrix} 3 \\ 2 \end{pmatrix}$ are (5, 3), (9, 3) and (9, 4).

2 a

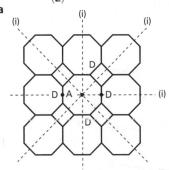

b Let x = interior angle of regular octagon
Angle sum at any vertex = $2x + 90° = 360°$
So $2x = 270°$ and $x = 135°$

page 121
1 a T_3 b T_4 c T_2 d T_1
2
$\overrightarrow{AB}$ → 3b
$\overrightarrow{PQ}$ → a − b
$\overrightarrow{BA}$ → $\frac{1}{2}$a
$\overrightarrow{EF}$ → a + b
$\overrightarrow{CD}$ → −2a
$\overrightarrow{XY}$ → 2a

3 $\overrightarrow{CD} = \begin{pmatrix} -2 \\ 2 \end{pmatrix}$, $\overrightarrow{BA} = \begin{pmatrix} -2 \\ 2 \end{pmatrix}$, i.e. they are parallel

$\overrightarrow{DA} = \begin{pmatrix} 3 \\ 1 \end{pmatrix}$, $\overrightarrow{CB} = \begin{pmatrix} 3 \\ 1 \end{pmatrix}$, i.e. they are parallel

$\overrightarrow{CD} = \overrightarrow{BA}$ and $\overrightarrow{DA} = \overrightarrow{CB}$, so ABCD is a parallelogram

Topic 13: Shapes and solids

page 127
1 a Triangular prism

b Cuboid

c Square-based pyramid

d Cube

2 a

Name of shape	No. of faces	No. of vertices	No. of edges
Cube	6	8	12
Cuboid	6	8	12
Triangular prism	5	6	9
Triangular pyramid	4	4	6
Square pyramid	5	5	8

b No. of faces + no. of vertices = no. of edges + 2
c No; e.g. cylinder

page 129
1 Sides of triangle 2.1 cm, 2.8 cm and 3.5 cm
$2.1^2 + 2.8^2 = 12.25$
$\sqrt{12.25} = 3.5$, so Pythagoras' theorem works.
2 a $w^2 = 1^2 + 1^2 = 2$
$w = \sqrt{2} = 1.41$ cm
b $x^2 = 2^2 + 7^2 = 53$
$x = \sqrt{53} = 7.28$ cm
c $y^2 = 7^2 - 3^2 = 40$
$y = \sqrt{40} = 6.32$ cm
d $z^2 = \frac{1}{2} \times 82 = 32$
$z = \sqrt{32} = 5.66$ cm
3 Let h = height of triangle
Then $10^2 = 5^2 + h^2$
$h^2 = 75$
$h = \sqrt{75} = 8.66$ cm (3 sf)

page 131
1 a AB = 1.73 cm (3 sf)
b CD = 3.46 cm (3 sf)
c EF = 5.20 cm (3 sf)
2 Height of pyramid = $\sqrt{82}$ = 9.06 cm (3 sf)
Volume of pyramid = $\frac{1}{3} \times (6 \times 6) \times \sqrt{82}$ = 108.66 ...
= 109 cm³ (3 sf)
3 Diagonal of cuboid = $(\sqrt{30^2 + 20^2 + 10^2})$ = $\sqrt{1400}$
= 37.4 cm (3 sf)

Topic 14: Triangles and quadrilaterals

page 137

1 a

b

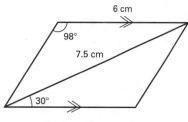

c

2 a Yes; all sides equal (SSS)
b Yes; right-angled, hypotenuse and one other side equal (RHS)
c No

3 Two triangles with the same angles as each other could be congruent.
Two triangles with the same length sides as each other must be congruent.
Two triangles with the same perimeter but different areas cannot be congruent.

4 $\dfrac{CD}{AB} = \dfrac{CO}{BO}$; $CD = \dfrac{CO}{BO} \times AB = \dfrac{15 \times 15}{12} = 18.75$ cm (2 dp)

page 139

1 a False   **c** False   **e** True
   b True   **d** True   **f** False

2 a $AD = \sqrt{13^2 - 12^2} = 5$ cm

   b $\cos \alpha = \dfrac{12}{13}$

   c $AB = 13 \div \cos \alpha = \dfrac{13^2}{12} = 14.1$ cm (3 sf)

   d $BC = \sqrt{(14.083\ldots^2 - 13^2)} = 5.42$ cm (3 sf)

3 Bearing of A from B = $180° + 60° = 240°$
Distance of C from A = $\sqrt{20^2 + 10^2} = \sqrt{500}$
$= 22.4$ km (3 sf)
$\tan C\hat{A}B = \frac{10}{20}$ so $C\hat{A}B = 26.56°$
Bearing of C from A = $60° - 26.56\ldots° = 33.43\ldots°$
$= 033.4°$ (3 sf)

page 141

1 a False   **b** True   **c** True   **d** True
2 a $x° = 80°$

   b $BD^2 = 10^2 + 9^2 - 2 \times 9 \times 10 \cos 80$
      $= 100 + 81 - 31.2566\ldots = 149.7433\ldots$
      $BD = \sqrt{149.7433\ldots} = 12.24$ cm

   c $\dfrac{\sin 80°}{12.24} = \dfrac{\sin A\hat{B}D}{9}$

      $\sin A\hat{B}D = \dfrac{9 \times \sin 80°}{12.24} = 0.7241$
      $A\hat{B}D = \sin^{-1} 0.7241 = 46.4°$ (3 sf)

3 $a^2 = 5^2 + 6^2 - 2 \times 5 \times 6 \cos 78.5°$
$a^2 = 25 + 36 - 11.9620\ldots = 49.0379\ldots$
$a^2 = 7$ cm
$\dfrac{5}{7.5} = \dfrac{6}{9} = \dfrac{7}{10.5}$
All three pairs of sides are in the same ratio, therefore A and B are similar
Area of $A = \frac{1}{2} \times 5 \times 6 \sin 78.5$
$= 15 \sin 78.5° = 14.7$ cm^2 (3 sf)
Area of $B = \frac{1}{2} \times 7.5 \times 9 \sin 78.5$
$= 33.75 \sin 78.5° = 33.1$ cm^2 (3 sf)

Topic 15: Measurement and drawings

page 147

1

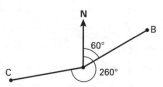

2 a B   **b** D   **c** C   **d** A
3 8 kilometres per hour; 5 miles per hour;
$\dfrac{8 \times 1000}{60} \times 60$ metres per second;
$\dfrac{8 \times 1000}{60}$ metres per minute
4 a $8 \text{ cm}^2 = 800 \text{ mm}^2$
   b $50 \text{ km}^2 = 50\,000\,000 \text{ m}^2$
   c $2.5 \text{ m}^2 = 25\,000 \text{ cm}^2$
   d $4 \text{ m}^3 = 4\,000\,000 \text{ cm}^3$
   e $1 \text{ cm}^3 = 1000 \text{ mm}^3$
   f $2.5 \text{ km}^3 = 2\,500\,000\,000 \text{ m}^3$
5 Bearing of A from B = $240°$

page 149

1

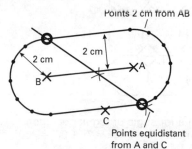

Points 2 cm from AB

Points equidistant from A and C

⦿ Points that satisfy both instructions

2

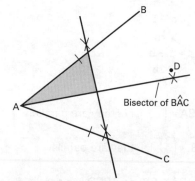

Bisector of B$\hat{A}$C

198

3 a

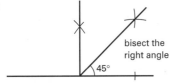

bisect the
right angle

45°

b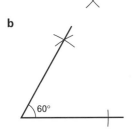

60°

c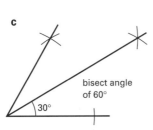

bisect angle
of 60°

30°

page 151
1 a $x = 30°, x = 150°$ **b** $x = 197°, x = 343°$
2 a

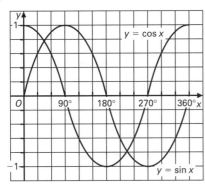

$y = \cos x$

$y = \sin x$

b $x = 45°, x = 225°$

Handling data

Topic 16: Collection and representation
page 159
1

Number	Tally	Frequency
1–5	卌 |||	8
6–10	卌 卌 |||	13
11–15	卌 卌 卌 卌 ||||	24
16–20	卌 卌 卌 ||	17
21–25	卌 卌 卌		16

2 a Total number of ice creams = 60
60 ice creams are represented by 360°
1 ice cream is represented by 360° ÷ 60 = 6°
Angle for vanilla   = 15 × 6 = 90°
Angle for strawberry = 18 × 6 = 108°
Angle for chocolate   = 16 × 6 = 96°
Angle for raspberry   = 11 × 6 = 66°
                           Total = 360°

b

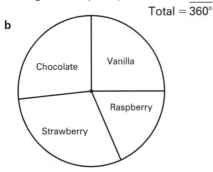

Chocolate

Vanilla

Raspberry

Strawberry

page 161
1 a Weak positive correlation
b Strong negative correlation
c No correlation
d Weak negative correlation
e Strong positive correlation

2

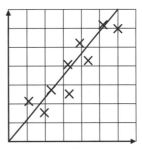

3 a 20 minutes
b 11 marks
c Answer **b** is more accurate as there are more
points plotted and the line is likely to be a better
fit in this area.

page 163
1 The areas of the bars on a histogram represent the
frequency, unlike the bars of a bar chart.
2

Duration of call (to nearest min.)	Frequency	Class width	Frequency density
1–3	18	3	18 ÷ 3 = 6
4–6	24	3	24 ÷ 3 = 8
7–12	20	6	20 ÷ 6 = $3\frac{1}{3}$
13–24	17	12	17 ÷ 12 = 1.42

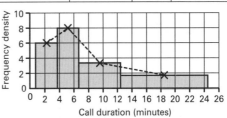

Call duration (minutes)

Topic 17: Averages and spread

page 171

1

fx	0	3	22	36	20	20	$\Sigma fx = 101$

$\text{Mean} = \dfrac{\Sigma fx}{\Sigma f} = \dfrac{101}{35} = 2.89$

Although the Mathematics marks have a greater
range than the English, the mean mark for both
tests is the same.

2

Cumulative frequency	0	3	14	26	31	35

See comment for question 1.

page 173
1 $\Sigma f = 46$

x	1	4	8	15	30	
fx	8	48	104	120	150	$\Sigma fx = 430$

$\text{Mean} = \dfrac{\Sigma fx}{\Sigma f} = \dfrac{430}{46} = 9.34\text{ cm}$ (3 sf)

2 a 28 minutes   **c** 33 minutes
b 20 minutes   **d** 13 minutes
IQR is a good measure of range because it
excludes rogue values.

1 $\sum f = 35$

fx	0	4	14	27	36	20	$\sum fx = 101$
fx^2	0	4	28	81	144	100	$\sum fx^2 = 357$

$\text{Mean} = \dfrac{\sum fx}{\sum f} = \dfrac{101}{35} = 2.89 \ (3 \text{ sf})$

$s = \sqrt{\dfrac{\sum fx^2}{\sum f} - \left(\dfrac{\sum fx}{\sum f}\right)^2} = \sqrt{\dfrac{357}{35} - \left(\dfrac{101}{35}\right)^2}$

$= 1.37 \ (3 \text{ sf})$

2 $\sum f = 46$

fx	8	48	104	40	150	$\sum fx = 350$
fx^2	8	192	832	1800	4500	$\sum fx^2 = 7332$

$\text{Mean} = 9.34 \, \text{cm} \ (3 \text{ sf})$
$s = 8.49 \, \text{cm} \ (3 \text{ sf})$

Topic 18: Probability

page 183

1 $1 - (0.45 + 0.2) = 0.35$

2

		Spinner		
	Red (R)	Yellow (Y)	Green (G)	Blue (B)
1	1, R	1, Y	1, G	1, B
2	2, R	2, Y	2, G	2, B
Dice 3	3, R	3, Y	3, G	3, B
4	4, R	4, Y	4, G	4, B
5	5, R	5, Y	5, G	5, B
6	6, R	6, Y	6, G	6, B

a $\dfrac{6}{24} = \dfrac{1}{4}$ **b** $\dfrac{4}{24} = \dfrac{1}{6}$ **c** $\dfrac{1}{24}$ **d** $\dfrac{1}{24}$

3 a

			Dice			
		1	2	3	4	5	6
Coin	H	2	4	6	8	10	12
	T	1	2	3	4	5	6

b i $\frac{1}{12}$ **ii** $\frac{9}{12} = \frac{3}{4}$ **iii** $\frac{1}{12}$
c Scores of 2, 4 and 6 are equally most likely

page 185

1 a Yes **b** No **c** Yes **d** No

2 Independent events do not affect each other, dependent events do.

3 a

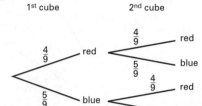

b i $\frac{4}{9} \times \frac{5}{9} = \frac{20}{81}$ **ii** $\frac{5}{9} \times \frac{5}{9} = \frac{25}{81}$ **iii** $\frac{4}{9} \times \frac{5}{9} + \frac{5}{9} \times \frac{4}{9} = \frac{40}{81}$

page 187

1 a

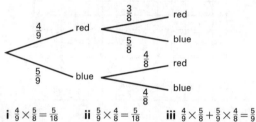

b i $\frac{4}{9} \times \frac{5}{8} = \frac{5}{18}$ **ii** $\frac{5}{9} \times \frac{4}{8} = \frac{5}{18}$ **iii** $\frac{4}{9} \times \frac{5}{8} + \frac{5}{9} \times \frac{4}{8} = \frac{5}{9}$

2 a $0.3 \times 0.1 = 0.03$

b $0.7 \times 0.6 = 0.42$

c $0.3 \times 0.9 + 0.7 \times 0.4 = 0.55$

Answers to Examination Questions

Number

Topic 1: The rules of number

1 a 0, 0.058, 0.085, 0.55, 0.555, 0.56, 1
  b i 0.54   **ii** 0.8

2 $\frac{120}{100} \times 15 = \frac{6}{5} \times 15 = 18$ oranges

3 a 1992 sale price is 87.5% (100% − 12.5%)
    of 1990 price
    1992 price = £88 000 × 0.875 = £77 000
  b 1996 sale price is 101.5% (100% + 1.5%)
    of 1990 price
    1996 price = £88 000 × 1.015 = £89 320
    Value of Elm Tree House has increased by
    £89 320 − £88 000 = £1320

4 21 × 65.9 p = 1383.9 p = £13.84 (to nearest penny)

5 $\frac{8}{4}$, 5

6 0.6, 0.666, 0.$\dot{6}$, 0.67, 0.7

7 a Fraction of arable land
$$= 1 - \left(\frac{1}{6} + \frac{5}{18}\right) = 1 - \left(\frac{3+5}{18}\right) = 1 - \frac{8}{18} = \frac{10}{18} = \frac{5}{9}$$
  b Area of arable land
$$= \frac{5}{9} \times 324 = 5 \times 36 = 180 \text{ hectares}$$

8 Discount = 13.80 − 12.30 = £1.50
  1.50 ÷ 13.80 = 0.1086 … = 11% (2 sf)

9 Sale price is 80% of original price
  1% of original price = £25 ÷ 80 = £0.3125
  100% of original price = 100 × £0.3125 = £31.25

10 Sale price is 90% of original price
  1% of original price = £32.40 ÷ 90 = £0.36
  100% of original price = 100 × £0.36 = £36

11 a $100x = 100 \times 0.\dot{4}\dot{5} = 45.\dot{4}\dot{5}$
  b $99x = 100x - x = 45.\dot{4}\dot{5} - 0.\dot{4}\dot{5} = 45$
  c $99x = 45$ so $x = \frac{45}{99} = \frac{5}{11}$
  d Let $y = 0.\dot{4}5\dot{6}$; $1000y = 456.\dot{4}5\dot{6}$
    $999y = 45.\dot{4}5\dot{6} - 0.\dot{4}5\dot{6} = 456$
$$y = \frac{456}{999} = \frac{152}{333}$$

12 a A rational number can be expressed in the form $\frac{a}{b}$
    where a and b are both integers
  b $(\sqrt{2} + \sqrt{8})^2 = (\sqrt{2})^2 + 2\sqrt{2}\sqrt{8} + (\sqrt{8})^2$
    $= 2 + 2\sqrt{16} + 8$
    $= 2 + 2 \times 4 + 8 = 18$
    or
    $\sqrt{2} + \sqrt{8} = \sqrt{2} + 2\sqrt{2} = 3\sqrt{2}$
    $(\sqrt{2} + \sqrt{8})^2 = (3\sqrt{2})^2 = 3^2 \times (\sqrt{2})^2 = 9 \times 2 = 18$
    Example:
  c $(2 + \sqrt{8})^2 = 12 + 8\sqrt{2}$ which is irrational

13 a i $x = \sqrt{(5^2 + 10^2)} = \sqrt{(25 + 100)}$
                $= \sqrt{125} = 5\sqrt{5}$ (irrational)
    ii $x = \sqrt{(3 + 6)} = \sqrt{9} = 3$ (rational)
  b Example: $a = \sqrt{3}, b = 1$ $(x = \sqrt{3 + 1} = \sqrt{4} = 2)$

14 $\sqrt{12} \times \sqrt{6} = \sqrt{72} = \sqrt{2 \times 36} = 6\sqrt{2}$

15 a i irrational   **ii** irrational
    iii rational: $3^0 + 3^{-1} + 3^{-2} = 1 + \frac{1}{3} + \frac{1}{9} = \frac{13}{9}$
  b Let $p = \sqrt{2}$ and $q = \sqrt{8}$, then $pq = \sqrt{2} \times \sqrt{8} = \sqrt{16} = 4$,
    which is rational
  c Let $x = 0.0\dot{3}\dot{6}$, $100x = 3.6\dot{3}\dot{6}$
    $99x = 3.6\dot{3}\dot{6} - 0.0\dot{3}\dot{6} = 3.6$
$$x = \frac{3.6}{99} = \frac{36}{990} = \frac{2}{55}$$

Topic 2: More number

1 a −8, −5, −2, −1, 0, 2, 4
  b −8 + −5 + −2 + −1 + 0 + 2 + 4 = −10

2 a 3 : 4
  b $\frac{3}{7} = 0.4285 \ldots = 43\%$ (2 sf) are girls

3 645 166 ÷ 4 = 161 291.5 = 161 000 (3 sf) people are
  retired

4 $\frac{3}{4} \times$ £80 million = £60 million was given to swimming

5 Distance travelled on 1 litre of diesel
  = 559 ÷ 53.7 = 10.4096 … = 10.4 miles (3 sf)

6 5 × −6 + −10 = −30 + −10 = −40

7 Time taken to deliver 1 litre = 20 ÷ 8 = 2.5 s
  Time taken to deliver 70 litres = 70 × 2.5 = 175 s
                          = 3 min 55 s

8 a 24.860 526 32
  b $\dfrac{4.7 \times 20.1}{5.6 - 1.8} \approx \dfrac{5 \times 20}{6 - 2} = \dfrac{80}{4} = 20$

9 a Gallons of petrol used = 7764 ÷ 37 = 209.837 …
    Litres of petrol used = 4.55 × 209.837 …
    Money spent on petrol = 52 × 4.55 × 209.837 …
    = 49 647.632 … p = £496.48 (to nearest penny)
  b Gallons of petrol used ≈ 8000 ÷ 40 = 200
    Litres of petrol used ≈ 200 × 5 = 1000
    Money spent on petrol ≈ 50 × 1000
                    = 50 000 p = £500

10 a Units used = $\dfrac{(42.91 - 10.33) \times 100}{749}$ = 434.979 …
              = 435 (nearest whole unit)
  b Total bill = quarterly charge + cost of electricity used
           = £10.33 + £(7.49 × 578 ÷ 100)
           = £10.33 + £43.2922
           = £53.62 (nearest penny)

11 Rounding to 1 sf, 876 ÷ 32 ≈ 900 ÷ 30 = 30

12 a 5   **b** −2

13 239.15 s

14 a Greatest weight = 20.5 kg; least weight 19.5 kg
  b Least possible weight of case = 19.35 kg
    So, greatest possible weight of sweater
    = 20.5 − 19.35 = 1.15 kg

15 Upper bound = (8 × 200.5) + (7 × 80.5)
              = 1604 + 563.5 = 2167.5 m
  Lower bound = (8 × 199.5) + (7 × 79.5)
              = 1596 + 556.5 = 2152.5 m

16 a Smallest possible area = 19.5 × 29.5 = 575.25 cm²
  b Largest possible area = $(x + 0.5)^2 = x^2 + x + 0.25$
    Smallest possible area = $(x - 0.5)^2 = x^2 - x + 0.25$
    Difference = $(x^2 + x + 0.25) - (x^2 - x + 0.25)$
           = $2x$ cm²

Topic 3: Describing number

1 Time taken for light to travel from nearest star
  = $4.0 \times 10^{13} \div 3.0 \times 10^5 = 1.33 \times 10^8$ s
$$1.3 \times 10^8 \text{ s} = \frac{1.3 \times 10^8}{60 \times 60 \times 24 \times 365}$$
$$= \frac{1.3 \times 10^8}{31\,536\,000} = 4.23 \text{ years (3 sf)}$$
  Distance to nearest star = 4.23 light years (3 sf)

2 Joseph

3 4, 16

4 a $2^5 = 2 \times 2 \times 2 \times 2 \times 2 = 32$
  b $5^2 = 25$
    Difference = 32 − 25 = 7

5 $\sqrt{5} - \sqrt[3]{10} = 2.236 \ldots - 2.1544 \ldots = 0.0816 \ldots$
  = 0.08 (2 dp)

6 Thickness of one sheet $= 5 \div 500 = 0.01 = 1 \times 10^{-2}$ cm

7 a $3^2 \times 3^5 = 3^{(2+5)} = 3^7$
  b $3^6 \div 3^2 = 3^{(6-2)} = 3^4$

8 a HCF of 216 and 168 is 24
  b 2.4 m

9 $\sqrt{200} = \sqrt{2 \times 100} = 10\sqrt{2}$
  $\sqrt[3]{2000} = \sqrt[3]{2 \times 1000} = 10\sqrt[3]{2}$
  $\sqrt{2} > \sqrt[3]{2}$ so $\sqrt{200} > \sqrt[3]{2000}$

10 a Percentage retired
    $= \dfrac{1.04 \times 10^7}{5.80 \times 10^7} \times 100 = 17.93 \ldots = 18\%$ (2 sf)

  b Population of Europe $= 0.138 \times 5.72 \times 10^9$
    $= 7.8936 \times 10^8 = 7.89 \times 10^8$ (3 sf)

11 a 3.5×10^{16} miles
  b Time taken $= \dfrac{3.5 \times 10^{16}}{5.9 \times 10^{12}} = 5932.20 \ldots$
    $= 6000$ years (1 sf)

12 a i $x = 4$ **ii** $y = -2$ **iii** $z = \frac{1}{3}$
  b $\sqrt{32} = \sqrt{2^5} = 2^{5/2}$

13 a $\dfrac{a^6 c^4}{a^2 c^5} = (a^{6-2})(c^{4-5}) = a^4 c^{-1} = \dfrac{a^4}{c}$
  b i $4^{-2} = \dfrac{1}{4^2} = \dfrac{1}{16}$ **ii** $8^{\frac{1}{3}} = \sqrt[3]{8} = 2$

14 $\sqrt{12} = \sqrt{3 \times 4} = 2\sqrt{3} = 2 \times 3^{\frac{1}{2}}$
  So $\dfrac{1}{\sqrt{12}} = (2 \times 3^{\frac{1}{2}})^{-1} = 2^{-1} \times 3^{-\frac{1}{2}}$
  Therefore $x = -\frac{1}{2}$

Topic 4: Application of number

1 a £450 $= 450 \times 3.4 = 1530$ Singapore Dollars
  b 27 Singapore Dollars $= 27 \div 3.4 = 7.94 \ldots$
    $= £8$ (nearest pound)

2 Small size: 1 m/ costs $50 \div 72 = 0.694$p
  Medium size: 1 m/ costs $90 \div 135 = 0.6$p
  Medium size is better value for money

3

x	5	10	20
y	45	180	720

4 28 m/s $= 28 \times 60 \times 60 = 100\,800$ m/h $= 100.8$ km/h
  $= 100$ km/h (2 sf)

5 Taxable income $= £27\,000 - £3525 = £23\,475$
  Tax paid at 20% $= 0.2 \times £3200 = £640$
  Tax paid at 25% $= 0.25 \times (£23\,475 - £3200) = £5068.75$
  Total tax paid $= £5068.75 + £640 = £5708.75$

6 a 2 hours 30 minutes $= 2.5$ hours
    Distance $= 2.5 \times 80 = 200$ miles
  b New journey time $= 200 \div 100 = 2$ hours
    So 30 minutes will be saved on journey time

7 $P = 66.2 \times 10^6 \left(1 + \dfrac{3}{100}\right)^5$
  $= 66.2 \times 10^6 \times 1.03^5 = 76.7 \times 10^6 = 76.7$ million

8 Volume $= 5 \times 5 \times 10 = 250$ cm^3
  Density $= 354$ g $\div 250$ cm$^3 = 1.416 = 1.42$ g/cm^3 (3 sf)

9 a $fw = k$, so $k = 1000 \times 300 = 300\,000 = 3 \times 10^5$
    When $f = 600$ kHz, $w = 3 \times 10^5 \div 600 = 500$ m
  b When $w = 842$ m, $f = 3 \times 10^5 \div 842 = 356.294 \ldots$
    $= 356.3$ kHz (4 sf)
  c If $f = w$, $w^2 = k$, so $w = \sqrt{k} = \sqrt{3 \times 10^5} = 547.72 \ldots$
    $= 547.7$ m (4 sf)

10 a $NL^2 = k$, where k is a constant
    $k = 2000 \times 0.4^2 = 320$
  b $N = k \div L^2 = 320 \div 0.6^2 = 888.88 \ldots$ 889 tiles

11 $yv = k$, so $k = 2 \times 3500 = 7000$
  a Value, v, of car after 5 years $= k \div y = 7000 \div 5$
    $= £1400$
  b Age y of car $= k \div v = 7000 \div 1000 = 7$ years

12 Time taken $= \dfrac{100}{30} = 3\frac{1}{3}$ hours $= 3$ hours 20 minutes

13 Volume $= 3 \times 5 \times 9 = 135$ cm^3
  Mass $=$ volume $\times$ density $= 135 \times 0.95 = 128.25$ g

Algebra

Topic 5: The language of algebra

1 a $-x + 13y$ **b** $2x + 10$
2 a $2x + 2y$ **b** $5pq$
3 $2x + 10 + 3x + x + 120 + 2x - 20 = 8x + 110$
4 a $(2x - 4)(x + 6) = 2x^2 + 12x - 4x - 24$
                $= 2x^2 + 8x - 24$
  b i $2x(x - 2y)$ **ii** $(x + 12)(x - 2)$
5 a $3x^3 - 5x$ **b** $6x^2 - x - 2$
6 a i $8y$ **ii** $6y + 6$ **iii** $y = 3$
  b $2x + 4 = 8x - 2$, $6x = 6$ ∴ $x = 1$
    Area of rectangle $= 2(x + 2) = 2 \times 3 = 6$ cm^2
7 a t^8 **b** p^4 **c** a^4

8 a $x^{-2}, \dfrac{1}{x}, x^{\frac{1}{2}}, x$ **b** $x, x^{\frac{1}{2}}, \dfrac{1}{x}, x^{-2}$

10 $\dfrac{1}{\sqrt{a}} = a^{-\frac{1}{2}}$; so $n = -\frac{1}{2}$

Topic 6: Making graphs

1 a

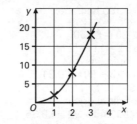

  b $x = 2.45$

2

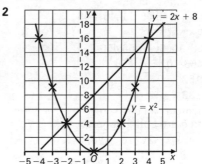

Points of intersection $(-2, 4)$ and $(4, 16)$

3

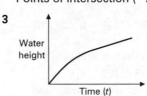

4 a i $y = 2f(x)$

ii $y = f(x - 1)$

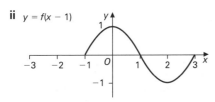

b C, $a = \frac{1}{2}$

Topic 7: Using graphs

1

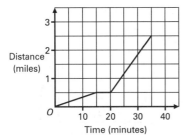

2 a, c

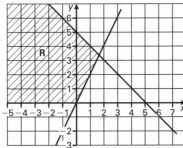

b The solution of the equation $2x = 5 - x$ is given by the x co-ordinate of the point of intersection of the two lines.

3 a

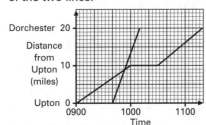

b 0954

4 $x = 1.5$

5 a 1st graph; $3x + 4y = p$: 2nd graph; $y = 3x - p$: 3rd graph; $y = px^3$

b $y = x^2 + p$

6 a See page 207 for answer

b $x^2 - 2x - 1 = 0$
$x^2 - 3x = -x + 1$
$x = -0.4$ or $x = 2.4$

c $x^2 - 3x \leqslant 1$
$-0.3 \leqslant x \leqslant 3.3$

7 a 2 m/s^2 **b** 34 m

8 a The train accelerates from rest for 40 s up to a steady speed of 30 m/s. It travels at constant speed for 20 s and then decelerates to rest for 40 s.

b Maximum acceleration $\approx 1.5 \text{ m/s}^2$

c Distance between stations $\approx 1950 \text{ m}$

9 a Acceleration at $t = 7.5$ is approximately 1.6 m/s^2

b 296 m

c Distance travelled in interval $0 \leqslant t \leqslant 10$

10 a i See page 208 for answer

ii $x = 114°$ or $x = 246°$

b i

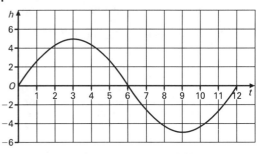

ii 4.3 m

Topic 8: Using algebra

1 $2(3x + 5) = 4x + 7$
$6x + 10 = 4x + 7$
$2x = -3$
$x = -1\frac{1}{2}$

2 a i Area of P $= 4 \times 2x = 8x \text{ cm}^2$

ii Perimeter of P $= 2x + 4 + 2x + 4 = 4x + 8 \text{ cm}$

b $4x + 8 = 12x + 2$
$8x = 6$
$x = \frac{3}{4}$

3 $h = ut + \frac{1}{2}at^2 = (12.9 \times 5) + (\frac{1}{2} \times -9.8 \times 5^2)$
$= 64.5 - 122.5 = -58 \text{ m}$

4 $x = 3, y = \frac{1}{2}$

5 $x = \dfrac{-b \pm \sqrt{b^2 - 4ac}}{2a} = \dfrac{2 \pm \sqrt{8}}{2}$

$x = 2.41$ or $x = -0.41$ (2 dp)

6 a Let y be width of rectangle, then $2y = 20 - 2x$ and $y = 10 - x$
Area of rectangle $= xy = x(10 - x)$
$x(10 - x) = 11$
$10x - x^2 + 11 = 0$
$x^2 - 10x + 11 = 0$

b $x = \dfrac{10 \pm \sqrt{100 - 44}}{2} = \dfrac{10 \pm \sqrt{56}}{2}$

$x = 8.74$ or $x = 1.26$
Length of rectangle $= 8.74 \text{ cm}$, width $= 1.26 \text{ cm}$ (2 dp)

Topic 9: More using algebra

1 50

2 a 38

b No. of outside edges $= 4n + 6$

3 a i n^2 **ii** $4n^2$

b For any number n, either $n + 1$ or $n + 2$ is an even number. An even number multiplied by an odd number is always even. Therefore every term in $(n + 1)(n + 2)$ must be even.

4 a 31

b $5n + 2$

c $n^2 + n$

5 $V = \frac{1}{3}\pi r^2 h$

$\dfrac{3V}{\pi h} = r^2$

$r = \sqrt{\dfrac{3V}{\pi h}}$

Value of x	Value of x^3	
2	8	too small
3	27	too big
2.8	21.952	too small
2.9	24.389	too big
2.85	23.149	too big

6 (header to left)

Solution lies between 2.8 and 2.85, so $x = 2.8$ (1 dp)

7

Value of x	Value of $x^3 - x$	Comment
3.5	39.375	too big
3.4	35.904	too big
3.3	32.637	too small
3.35	34.245	too small

Solution lies between 3.35 and 3.4, so $x = 3.4$ (1 dp)

8 a i $2r(r + h)$ **ii** $2x^2 - 5x - 12$

   b i $b = 75$ **ii** $M = b + \sqrt{\dfrac{P}{a}}$

9 $l = \dfrac{p - 6}{p + 2}$

   $lp + 2l = p - 6$
   $lp - p = -2l - 6$
   $p(l - 1) = -2l - 6$

      $p = \dfrac{-2l - 6}{l - 1} = \dfrac{2l - 6}{1 - l}$

Shape, Space and Measures

Topic 10: Angle properties

1 a $p = 56°$, $q = 124°$
   b $r = s = 60°$
   c $t = 102°$
2 a i obtuse angle   **ii** isosceles
   b $35°$
   c $35°$, $\widehat{CDP}$ and $\widehat{BPD}$ are alternate angles
3 $x = 117°$, $y = 27°$
4 a i trapezium   **ii** $x = 30°$
   b $y = 60°$ **c** $720°$
5 a $x = \dfrac{360}{8} = 45°$ **b** $y = \frac{1}{2}(180 - 45) = 67.5°$
6 a $32°$ **b** $64°$ **c** $90°$ **d** $58°$
7 a $\widehat{CBD} = \widehat{CAD}$ (subtended by chord CD)
     $\widehat{BDA} = \widehat{BCA}$ (subtended by chord AB)
     $\widehat{BXC} = \widehat{AXD}$ (opposite angles)
     So $\triangle BXC$ and $\triangle AXD$ are similar (equiangular)
   b 8.75 cm
8 a $100°$ **b** $84°$

Topic 11: Length, area and volume

1 12 000 cm³ (or 12 l)
2 Area $= \pi r^2 = \pi \times 7.5^2 = 176.7$ cm² (1 dp)
3 a Volume $= \frac{1}{3}\pi r^2 h + \frac{1}{2}(\frac{4}{3}\pi r^3) = \frac{1}{3}\pi r^2(h + 2r)$
      $= 497$ cm³ (3 sf)
   b Slant height of cone, $l = \sqrt{9^2 + 5^2} = 10.295 \ldots$
     Surface area $= \pi r l + \frac{1}{2}(4\pi r^2) = \pi r(l + 2r)$
      $= 319$ cm² (3 sf)
4 a i Circumference $= \pi d = \pi \times 7 = 22.0$ cm (1 dp)
   ii Area $= \pi r^2 = 38.5$ cm² (1 dp)
   b Volume $= \dfrac{\pi d^2 h}{4} = 38.5 \times 10 = 385$ cm³ (3 sf)
5 Area of A $= 4.5 \times 5 = 22.5$ cm²
   Area of B $= \dfrac{4.5}{2}(2.1 + 8) = 22.7$ cm² (1 dp)
   Shape B has the larger area

6 Area of base $= 1000 \div 20 = 50$ cm²
   $r^2 = \dfrac{50}{\pi} = 15.915\ldots$ so $r = \sqrt{15.915\ldots} = 3.98$ cm (3 sf)
7 Area of parallelogram $= 6 \times 3 = 18$ cm²
   Volume of ice cream $= 18 \times 12 = 216$ cm³
8 a AB $= 2 \times 5 \cos 30° = 5\sqrt{3} = 8.7$ cm (1 dp)
   b Shaded region $= \frac{1}{3}$(area of circle $-$ area of triangle)
      $= \frac{1}{3}(78.54 - 32.48) = 15.38$ cm² (1 dp)
9 Angle subtended at O by arc $= 90°$
   Area of sector $= \frac{1}{4} \times \pi \times (3.5^2 + 3.5^2) = 19.24$ m²
   Area of triangles $= 3.5 \times 3.5 = 12.25$ m²
   Total area $= 19.24 + 12.25 = 31.49$ m²

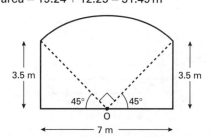

10 a ACB $= \frac{7}{8} \times \pi \times 40 = 15.71$ cm (2 dp)
   b i $15.71 = 2\pi r$ so $r = \dfrac{15.71}{2\pi} = 2.50$ cm
     ii Height of cone $= \sqrt{20^2 - 2.5^2} = 19.84$ cm
     Volume of cone $= \frac{1}{3} \times \pi \times 2.5^2 \times 19.84$
      $= 129.87$ cm³

Topic 12: Symmetry and transformations

1 a Reflection in the x axis
   b Rotation 90° anticlockwise about (0, 0)
   c Enlargement, scale factor 3, centre (5, 4)
2 a i Rotation   **ii** Translation
   b

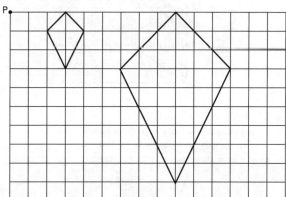

3 a, b, c i
c ii 1

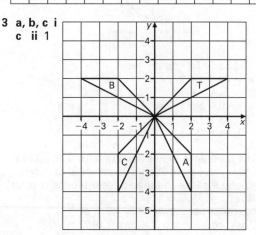

4 a

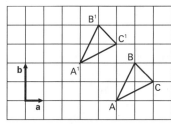

b i $\overrightarrow{AB} = \mathbf{a} + \mathbf{b}$ **ii** $\overrightarrow{BC} = \mathbf{a} - \frac{1}{2}\mathbf{b}$

c $\overrightarrow{BD} = \frac{2}{3}(\mathbf{a} - \frac{1}{2}\mathbf{b}) = \frac{2}{3}\mathbf{a} - \frac{1}{3}\mathbf{b}$

$\overrightarrow{AD} = \overrightarrow{AB} + \overrightarrow{BD}$

$= \mathbf{a} + \mathbf{b} + \frac{2}{3}\mathbf{a} - \frac{1}{3}\mathbf{b} = \frac{5}{3}\mathbf{a} + \frac{2}{3}\mathbf{b}$

$x = \frac{5}{3}, y = \frac{2}{3}$

5 a $\overrightarrow{RQ} = \mathbf{x} - \mathbf{y}$

b i $\overrightarrow{NM} = \overrightarrow{NL} + \overrightarrow{LM} = \mathbf{b} - \mathbf{a} + \mathbf{a} + 2\mathbf{b} = 3\mathbf{b}$

ii $3\mathbf{b} = \begin{pmatrix} 6 \\ 9 \end{pmatrix}$ so $\mathbf{b} = \begin{pmatrix} 2 \\ 3 \end{pmatrix}$

$\mathbf{a} = \begin{pmatrix} 5 \\ -4 \end{pmatrix} + \begin{pmatrix} 2 \\ 3 \end{pmatrix} = \begin{pmatrix} 7 \\ -1 \end{pmatrix}$

Topic 13: Shapes and solids

1

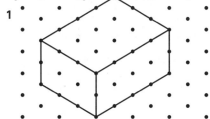

2 a

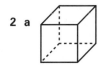

b B and C

3 Height $= \sqrt{2.75^2 - 1.80^2} = 2.08\,\text{m}$ (3 sf)

4 b i Area $= \frac{1}{2}\pi r^2 = 14.14\,\text{cm}^2$ (2 dp)

ii PY $= \sqrt{6^2 + 4^2} = 7.21\,\text{cm}^2$ (2 dp)

5 a i AC $= 2 \times \sqrt{10^2 - 6^2} = 16\,\text{m}$

ii Area of ABC $= \frac{1}{2} \times 16 \times 6 = 48\,\text{m}^2$

b Volume of roof space $= 48 \times 25 = 1200\,\text{m}^3$

6 a $x = 0.8 + \sqrt{4^2 - 0.7^2} = 4.7\,\text{m}$ (1 dp)

b Area of cross-section $= \frac{0.7}{2}(0.8 + 4.7) = 1.925\,\text{m}^2$

Volume $= 1.925 \times 1.5 = 2.9\,\text{m}^3$ (1 dp)

7 a AC $= \sqrt{5^2 + 5^2} = \sqrt{50} = \sqrt{2 \times 25} = 5\sqrt{2}\,\text{cm}$

AG $= \sqrt{5^2 + 5^2 + 5^2} = \sqrt{75} = \sqrt{3 \times 25} = 5\sqrt{3}\,\text{cm}$

Topic 14: Triangles and quadrilaterals

1 a $29°$ **b** $y = 4.5\,\text{cm}$

2 a BC $= 3.2 \cos 49° = 2.10\,\text{m}$ (1 dp)

b CD $= \dfrac{4.1}{\sin 58°} = 4.83\,\text{m}$ (1 dp)

3 a AB $= 10 \tan 32.6 = 6.4\,\text{m}$ (1 dp)

b $\overset{\wedge}{KTA} = \cos^{-1}\dfrac{10}{27} = 68.3°$ (1 dp)

4 $\dfrac{AB}{XY} = \dfrac{LA}{LX}$ so AB $= \dfrac{LA}{LX} \times XY = \dfrac{3 \times 6}{8} = 2.25\,\text{cm}$

5 $\dfrac{\sin 100°}{7} = \dfrac{\sin \overset{\wedge}{ABC}}{4}$ so $\sin \overset{\wedge}{ABC} = \dfrac{4 \sin 100°}{7}$

$= 0.5627\ldots$

$\overset{\wedge}{ABC} = 34.25°$ (4 sf)

Therefore $\overset{\wedge}{CAB} = 180 - 100 - 34.25 = 45.75°$ (4 sf)

Area of triangle $= \frac{1}{2} \times 4 \times 7 \sin 45.75°$

$= 10.028\ldots = 10.0\,\text{cm}^2$ (3 sf)

6 a $\frac{1}{2} \times 7 \times 8 \sin 100° = 27.57\,\text{cm}^2$ (2 dp)

b $BD^2 = 7^2 + 8^2 - (2 \times 7 \times 8 \cos 100°)$

$= 113 + 19.448\ldots = 132.448\ldots$

BD $= 11.51\,\text{cm}$ (2 dp)

c $\cos \overset{\wedge}{BCD} = \dfrac{5^2 + 6.8^2 - 11.5^2}{2 \times 5 \times 6.8} = -0.8972$

$\overset{\wedge}{BCD} = \cos^{-1} -0.8972 = 153.8°$ (1 dp)

Topic 15: Measurement and drawing

1 a $300°$

b i $4 \times 30 = 120\,\text{km}$ **ii** $120 \times \frac{5}{8} = 75\,\text{miles}$

2 a i $8.4 \times 5 = 42.0\,\text{km}$

ii Time taken $= 42/18 = 2\frac{1}{3}$ hours

$= 2$ hours 20 minutes

Brian arrives at $0930 + 0220 = 1150$

b

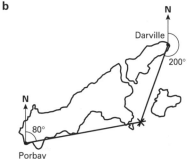

3

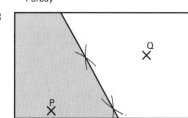

4 a i $\overset{\wedge}{BWH} = \sin^{-1}\dfrac{72}{86} = 56.8°$

ii $\overset{\wedge}{HBW} = 33.2°$

Bearing of B from W $= 45° - 33.2° = 011.8°$

b

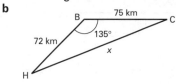

$x^2 = 75^2 + 72^2 - (2 \times 72 \times 75 \cos 135°)$

$= 18\,445.75\ldots$

$x = 135.815\ldots = 136\,\text{km}$ (3 sf)

5

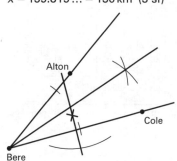

6 a $a = 2, b = -90°$
b $x = \sin^{-1}\frac{2}{3} = 41.8°, 138.2°$
7 a i $p = 330°$ **ii** $q = 30°$ or $q = 150°$
b

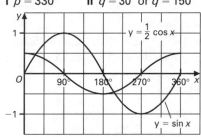

c $\sin x = \frac{1}{2}\cos x, x = 26.6°, 206.6°$

Topic 16: Collection and representation

1

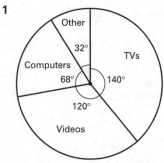

2 a

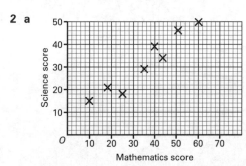

b Strong positive correlation
3 a There is strong negative correlation; the higher the rainfall, the fewer deck chair tickets sold.
b

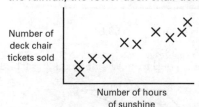

4 a

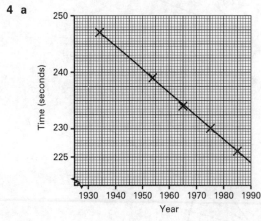

b 227 s

5 a

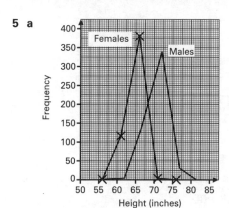

b Female heights have lower modal class and smaller range than male heights
6 a No. of pupils = $10 \times 1.6 = 16$
b Modal range is $60-80\%$

7 a

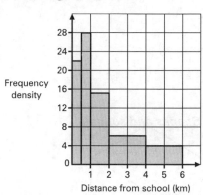

b i Mix of ages, socio-economic group, ability, sexes
ii Mix of ages: changes in selection criteria may mean that the size of catchment area differs between year groups.

Topic 17: Averages and spread

1 a i Range = $39 - 27 = 12$ **ii** Mean length = 32 cm
b Spanish cucumbers are generally shorter than English cucumbers and have less variation in their lengths.
2 Estimated mean travelling time
$$= \frac{\Sigma(f \times \text{mid-interval value})}{\Sigma f}$$
$$= 22.34775 = 22 \text{ minutes (to nearest minute)}$$
3 a i Modal class = 6–10
ii Median (50th value) is in class interval 11–15
b Mean $= \dfrac{\Sigma(f \times \text{mid-interval value})}{\Sigma f}$
$$= \frac{1487}{100}$$
$$= 14.87 \text{ words}$$
4 a *See page 208 for answer*
b $100 - 92 = 8$
c i Median = 25 hours
ii IQR = $27 - 23.5 = 3.5$
d No: because IQR is larger the battery lifetimes are more spread.
5 a Median finishing time = 101 minutes
b IQR = $103 - 89 = 14$ minutes

6 a Mean = 1.4 days, Standard deviation = 1.10 (3 sf)
 b Mean and standard deviation for 2nd class letters are both higher – so it is worth sending letters first class if you want them to get there quicker.
 c Mean is increased by 1 to 4.1 days; Standard deviation is unchanged
7 a Mean = 493.5, Standard deviation = 10.59 (4 sf)
 b If all readings are 10 too high, then mean is 10 too high
 So true mean
 = original mean − 10 = 493.5 − 10 = 483.5
 The fault does not affect the standard deviation.

Topic 18: Probability

1 a $\frac{1}{20}$ **b** $\frac{7}{20}$ **c** $\frac{13}{20}$
2 a $\frac{12}{20} = \frac{3}{5}$
 b

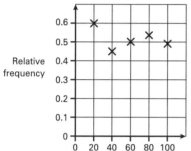

 c 0.5
3 a

	2	3	4	5	6
1	3	4	5	6	7
2	4	5	6	7	8
3	5	6	7	8	9
4	6	7	8	9	10
5	7	8	9	10	11

 b i $\frac{1}{25}$ **ii** $\frac{6}{25}$

4 a 0.05
 b

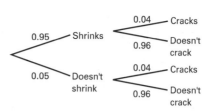

 c $0.95 \times 0.04 = 0.038$
5 a $\frac{6}{20} = \frac{3}{10}$
 b $\frac{7}{10}$
6 a $0.4 \times 0.2 = 0.08$
 b $0.4 \times 0.8 = 0.32$
 c $0.6 \times 0.8 = 0.48$
 d $0.4 \times 0.8 + 0.6 \times 0.2 = 0.32 + 0.12 = 0.44$
7

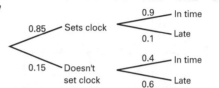

 $P(\text{gets up in time}) = 0.85 \times 0.9 + 0.15 \times 0.4$
 $= 0.765 + 0.06 = 0.825$
8 a $\dfrac{5}{20} \times \dfrac{4}{19} = \dfrac{20}{380} = \dfrac{1}{19}$
 b i $\frac{8}{19}$ **ii** $\frac{6}{19}$
 c $P(\text{each will have a different centre})$
 $= 6 \times \left(\dfrac{5 \times 7 \times 8}{20 \times 19 \times 18} \right) = \dfrac{1680}{6840} = \dfrac{14}{57}$

Topic 7 Question 6 a

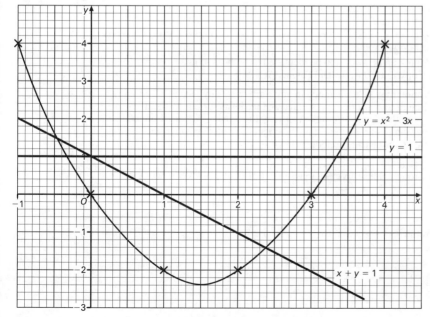

Topic 7 Question 10 a i

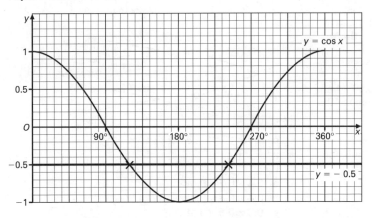

Topic 17 Question 4 a

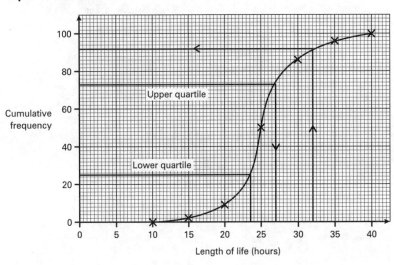

Acknowledgements

The publishers thank the following Examination Boards for permission to reproduce copyright material:

Southern Examining Group (SEG)
Northern Examinations and Assessment Board (NEAB)

Thanks to Tony Banks and John Readman for their invaluable contributions at review.
Thanks to the team at Stanley Thornes, in particular Adrian Wheaton, Malcolm Tomlin and Lorna Godson.

• •

First published 1999 by
Stanley Thornes (Publishers) Ltd, Ellenborough House, Wellington Street, CHELTENHAM GL50 1YW

ISBN 0 7487 4455 X

Typeset by Tech Set Ltd, Gateshead

Printed and bound in Spain by Mateu Cromo